FOCUSED for GOLF

WAYNE GLAD, PhD

CHIP BECK

Human Kinetics

Library of Congress Cataloging-in-Publication Data

Glad, Wayne, 1950-
    Focused for golf / Wayne Glad, Chip Beck
      p. cm.
    Includes index.
    ISBN 0-88011-857-1
    1. Golf--Psychological aspects.   I. Beck, Chip, 1956-
II. Title
GV979.P75G53   1999
796.352'01'9--dc21
                                                          98-40338
                                                                  CIP
ISBN: 0-88011-857-1

Acquisitions Editor: Martin Barnard; **Developmental Editor:** Kent Reel; **Assistant Editors:** Rebecca Crist and Kim Thoren; **Copyeditor:** John Wentworth; **Proofreader:** Myla Smith; **Indexer:** Joan Griffitts; **Graphic Designer:** Nancy Rasmus; **Graphic Artist:** Tom Roberts; **Photo Editor:** Boyd LaFoon; **Cover Designer:** Jack Davis; **Photographer (cover):** Jules Alexander; **Printer:** Versa Press

Human Kinetics books are available at special discounts for bulk purchases. Special editions or book excerpts can also be created to specification. For details, contact the Special Sales Manager at Human Kinetics.

Printed in the United States of America   10 9 8 7 6 5 4 3 2 1

Human Kinetics
Web site: http:// www.humankinetics.com/

United States: Human Kinetics
P.O. Box 5076, Champaign, IL 61825-5076
1-800-747-4457
e-mail: humank@hkusa.com

Canada: Human Kinetics
475 Devonshire Road Unit 100
Windsor, ON N8Y 2L5
1-800-465-7301 (in Canada only)
e-mail: humank@hkcanada.com

Europe: Human Kinetics
P.O. Box IW14,
Leeds LS16 6TR, United Kingdom
(44) 1132 781708
e-mail: humank@hkeurope.com

Australia: Human Kinetics
57A Price Avenue
Lower Mitcham, South Australia 5062
(088) 277 1555
e-mail: humank@hkaustralia.com

New Zealand: Human Kinetics
P.O. Box 105-231, Auckland 1
(09) 523 3462
e-mail: humank@hknewz.com

contents

foreword

Whenever I am given an opportunity to lecture or consult with groups of golfers, the very first question that I ask is, "What percentage of your golf game do you perceive to be mental?" The next question that I ask is, "How much of your training time do you devote to the mental game of golf?" Invariably, the second number is much smaller than the first. This comes despite the plethora of research evidence that shows the very real benefits that golfers obtain from very simple mental skills training. Some would rather hit golf balls for hours than train their minds for only a few minutes. Others do not believe that mental training works. Still others simply have no idea what mental training really is and how they would go about such training. Once this training is undertaken, typically in conjunction with swing lessons, I have seen the evidence that this methodology really works. In my practice, I have worked one-on-one with some of the best adult professional and amateur juniors in the world. With this type of training, coupled with a willingness to practice the techniques, players have shaved several strokes off their handicaps in short order.

Dr. Wayne Glad and Chip Beck have combined to write a book that contains proven tools that will enhance any golfer's ability to use his or her mind to play the game more effectively. At the David Leadbetter Golf Academies (and, for that matter, at the Bollettieri Tennis Academies with aspiring elite tennis players), we have seen the impact of these principles: Developing pre-shot routines; training the "all-around" athlete; building skills technically, mentally, and physically; overcoming pressure and slumps, etc. Using methods such as those outlined in this book, we have helped some of our junior golfers and other athletes to rise through the ranks to become top 10 players nationally and internationally.

Although there are many books on sports psychology and mental training, *Focused for Golf* stands out because of its practical approach which can be integrated into your golf game today regardless of your handicap or talent level. The many anecdotes throughout the book illustrate the effectiveness of this approach and also reinforce the now-recognized reality that mental training in conjunction with golf instruction is the optimal method for achieving your peak golf potential. Perhaps most important, this approach is outlined in an easy to understand manner, and encourages a proactive approach to preventing problems on the course before they occur.

There aren't many golfers who have more credibility than Chip Beck, both as a person and a professional. Beck's willingness to share his trials and undertakings, his struggles and his fixes, are among the highlights of a thoughtful and very helpful book. Dr. Wayne Glad's professional training, and his expertise and experience helping many elite athletes, including our juniors at the Leadbetter Golf Academy in Illinois, qualifies him to help you with your game whether you play golf daily or with less frequency. Ultimately this book will help you enjoy your golf game more, which may be the most valuable gift that Beck and Glad bring to you. I strongly urge you to get *Focused for Golf* and prepare to play the best golf of your life.

Jeff Troesch
Sport Psychologist
David Leadbetter Golf Academies
Bollettieri Tennis Academies
International Management Group (IMG)

introduction

It probably comes as no surprise to the frequent golfer that several professional golfers have gone on record with their belief that playing golf is between 80 and 90 percent mental and the rest physical or mechanical. For amateurs, the mental component perhaps is not quite as important as it is for the professional since the Nick Faldos, Tiger Woods, and Laura Davies of the world have their basic mechanics down and most amateurs don't. However, it still may surprise the amateur golfer how much scoring improvement can occur by working on the mental game.

This book was written by two golfers—one of them a pro with 18 years' experience, and the other still very much an amateur. The latter, however, has worked on performance enhancement with many of the best professional, collegiate, and high school golfers in the world to determine what it really takes to improve a golf game. The amateur golfer is also a licensed clinical psychologist who has spent the last 20-odd years helping people develop better skills in a variety of life areas, many of which directly apply to improving play on the golf course.

We have come together, a PGA tour golfer and a clinical and sport psychologist, to put together what each of us knows about improving performance to help the golfer who is seriously trying to get better. We feel that golf is a very difficult game to play well. Before we even get started, our first suggestion is that you accompany the purchase of this book with a few basic golf lessons, if you have not already had lessons. The combination of the lessons and the book should significantly help your play and improve the quality of your experience on the course.

We all have seen what a poor round of golf can do to a person who otherwise seems very nice and stable. We have seen thrown clubs, dogs kicked, and whole weekends ruined by a triple bogey on 18 that spoiled an otherwise great round. We all have had to endure the stories of the putt that should have dropped, the unfair lie, and the "rub of the green" as professional players call it, which is the Murphy's Law for golfers—if something *can* go wrong on the course or on the shot, it *will* go wrong.

Our goal in this project is not to add yet one more golf improvement book to your shelf but to give you and all golfers a blueprint for golf performance enhancement leading to totally *satisfying* golf. Unlike tour professionals who may not be satisfied until they win a major tournament, most amateurs want to develop their golf skills to play at a level that makes them happy, that makes it gratifying to step onto a golf course for three to four hours of enjoyment.

We will have succeeded in our goals if this book becomes for you a mental and physical skill-building resource, a book that you go to when you want to try something new to improve your golf, and return to for help if your game is "going south." We hope to remind you that the main goals of the game should be to help yourself grow and develop skills. If it occurs to you as you use the book for golf that the techniques discussed here also apply to other activities, then that's a bonus for us.

We realize that our goals for the book are lofty, but we have set our sights high in most of our other life areas also, and we believe that we have accomplished much of what we wanted to in this book. By the time you have finished reading it, we hope you feel the same way.

The structure of our book is simple and consistent throughout. Each chapter begins with an anecdote from Chip or another prominent player that happened in the world of professional golf. Each deals with an issue relating to mental skills and performance that will be the topic of that chapter. Then, early in each chapter, we introduce the chapter's "key principle," which will be the focus for the remainder of the chapter. The principles involve motivation, goal setting, the importance of establishing routines, boosting confidence, staying in control, performing under pressure, coping with slumps, and developing positive competitiveness.

An important bonus of this book is that in addition to drawing on Chip's 18 years on the PGA tour, we have solicited opinions and attitudes of other veteran tour players who comment on how important these issues are in golf and how they deal with them on the tour.

Each chapter then proceeds with our repertoire of techniques and skills jointly developed by the authors for you to learn and master. Many chapters also include exercises and drills to help you learn the skills and techniques. Some chapters end with worksheets to make it easier for you to start working on the skills right away.

Not all golfers have difficulties in all the areas we cover, so after reading the book through once you might want to focus on the chapters that will help you most. Because of the range of topics we cover, we're sure there's something here for everyone. OK, that's all we've got here, so turn the page and get started on building your mental skills for golf!

Setting Your Course

Taking Steps to Change

Chip Beck

When I first met with Dr. Glad, I had a clear sense of my wants and little difficulty organizing them into specific goals. First, I wanted assistance preparing for the four major tournaments in professional golf–the U.S. Open, the British Open, the PGA Championship, and the Masters. I felt that I was more tense before these tournaments than other tour events. I recognized that I was still responding to the majors in the way I had responded to *all* tour events early in my career, before I had gained considerable experience. Over the years on the tour, I had developed confidence during most of the other tour events, but perhaps in part because victory had eluded me at the majors I often played tight during these tournaments which surely

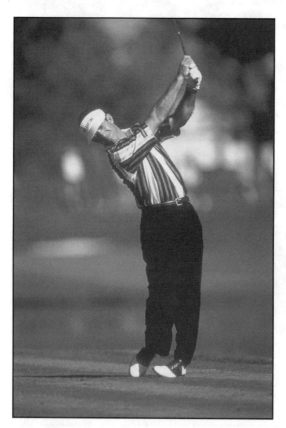

contributed to poor shot making, poor course management, and poor decisions. I hoped some sessions with Dr. Glad would help me develop anxiety management skills during the majors and other pressurized moments on the PGA tour.

Along with improving my play in the majors, another goal in meeting with Dr. Glad was to increase my ability to concentrate on the shot and hole at hand, to stop fretting over past poor shots and worrying about difficult shots or holes ahead. Sport psychologists refer to this as a problem with "staying in the present." It was a problem I had in the present, and I hoped to put it in my past.

In addition to my performance goals, I had some general "life goals" that I felt, if reached, would help my performance overall and in tournaments. One goal was learning how to be happier in a high-stress occupation. Others were to better blend my golf career with my family life (my wife, Karen, and I have four young children) and to learn to adjust to the many life changes I was undergoing as I approached middle age and more than 15 years on the PGA tour. I knew that I needed to adjust my game mentally and physically, to take into account my age and increasing off-the-course commitments. When I started working with Dr. Glad, I began a step-by-step plan to try to make the changes I desired in my golf game.

Making Positive Change

"Change" is one of those words that produces a surprisingly large range of responses in different people, and even different reactions in the same person at different times. Psychologists know that it is during times of great change that people experience the most stress and distress. We also know that it is during periods of change or transition that people have the greatest opportunity to grow, develop, and improve in life's endeavors. Sport psychologists recognize change as both adversity and opportunity. In sport and exercise, change presents adversity that must be tackled and overcome, but it also presents opportunity to reach the next level of performance. To make changes and achieve your goals, you need *motivation*, a key ingredient to any achievement or action.

KEY PRINCIPLE: MOTIVATION

A key principle for making positive change is developing a thoughtfully constructed, organized, and step-by-step program that, when carried out with effort and discipline, leads to successful change in golf performance. In most cases this change takes great patience, and it always takes hard work and commitment to the plan.

Being sufficiently motivated to work to become a better golfer is only the first step toward change. *Patience* is also crucial for a player desiring golf improvement: patience enough to practice regularly and frequently, and patience enough to "overlearn" the skill that you hope will enhance your game. It amazes us that even at the highest level of golf—the PGA tour—some players have trouble waiting for their first win, to make their first cut, or to earn their tour playing card.

Inner Motivation

Chip Beck

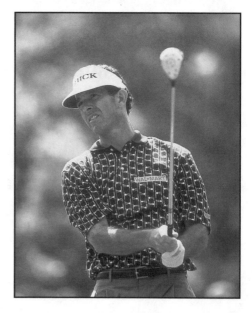

I grew up playing golf. And all the time I was playing, I was also looking forward to playing better and better golf. As I grew up, I was fortunate to play with many good golfers; most went on to college with golf scholarships. I looked forward to that myself. But I think my biggest goal was getting to the tour and playing golf for a living.

To achieve this goal I focused on the mental side of the game and worked hard to stay motivated. Some constant motivators for me are recognizing how much I have learned from playing golf, how much of my growth has occurred on the golf course or as a result of golf-related experiences, and that continuing to play golf will give me more of these opportunities. At my first pee-wee tournament, for instance, I felt that I worked all that summer playing and practicing, and I just enjoyed the game so much. Winning the tournament was a huge thrill for me and inspired me to keep going. At that point the process was under way. I had taken the first step toward my goal.

When I need motivation I think of that tournament and picture how I played and felt. I can still see that beautiful trophy in my mind. So many times I have taken myself back to that first tournament to relive the moment and relish it all over again.

Another early motivator in my life was meeting Raymond Floyd and Jack Nicklaus when they came to my hometown the first year I played golf. I was inspired just seeing them and what they could do. I think that was when I first began to know that I wanted to golf for the rest of my life. Later I was motivated by my Ryder Cup experiences. Once you've been involved in the Ryder Cup, you always want to go back. Maybe one reason I have attained it several times is that I use my past experience as a motivator, though I try not to put too much pressure on myself or let a fear of not attaining it disrupt my game.

I may be fortunate in the area of motivation because I am also motivated by things and people in my life that have value and a tendency to endure. The latest motivation in my life has been setting up the Chip Beck Scholarship Foundation and working with the charities my family is involved with. Being motivated by these kinds of things that last makes it easier to continue to perform, even during temporary setbacks. Motivation has been central to the successes I've had in golf and in life.

MOTIVATION PRESCRIPTION

- Develop a "motivation meter"
- Set performance goals using "Glad's GUIDES"

Checking Your Motivation Meter

Because high motivation is a necessary ingredient for successful change, our first prescription for setting your course is to develop a motivation meter. You can check this meter to see if you want something badly enough to put out enough effort over a long enough period to bring about change. You check the meter by paying attention to what you are thinking and feeling while you are going through various experiences, "reading" your level of motivation in several different experiences, and making a scale of motivation out of this exercise. For instance, think about the thing that you would most want to do and give that level of motivation the highest number, a 10. Next, consider something that you would least want to do of all things that you can think of and mark that level of motivation with a 0. Next, think of several other experiences and rate each one from 0 to 10 on how motivated you would be to do or experience them.

Now consider the golf performance change you would like to make and rate your motivation for it on the scale. Compare it with other items on the scale to help you better gauge the level of motivation. If you rate your motivation for attempting the change somewhere between 0 and 3, it is not likely that you will follow through. The change will require effort, practice, and patience, and you likely won't be up to it. You may as well postpone this change effort and choose another aspect of your game to improve. On the other hand, if your motivation for the change effort ranks high (7-10), you can reasonably expect to have the energy and drive to develop and carry out the change effort and the patience to wait for its payoff.

Setting Performance Goals With GUIDES

Once you have determined that you're sufficiently motivated to build your golf skills and improve your performance, the next thing you need is a method. In our work with other golfers and clients we have developed a sequence of activities that, if carried out, assures a serious effort at attempting change. The process begins with goal setting and is followed by understanding and awareness, implementation, disciplined practice, evaluation, and, finally, satisfaction and reward.

GLAD'S GUIDES

Goal setting
Understanding and awareness
Implementation
Disciplined practice
Evaluation
Satisfaction and reward

Before we discuss how to use GUIDES to gain positive changes, we'll briefly describe each of the six steps, with examples to help you apply the process to your own change efforts.

Goal Setting

The first step in GUIDES is *goal setting*. When you are interested in producing change, you need to start with clear-cut goals. Many athletes come to us with no defined goals in mind. Often they'll say they wish "to perform better," but they will not have thought through exactly what they want to accomplish.

What are some useful goals for golfers? One would be to achieve a higher specified standard of proficiency or, said another way, a specified greater skill level in a specific aspect of golf within a set amount of time. An example would be to say, "My goal is to be hitting 75% of greens in regulation by the end of the golf season." A more short-term goal might be, "I will use my pre-shot routine on every shot during today's round."

Short-term goals are more specific and generally easier to reach; long-term goals are broader and often require the successful completion of several short-term goals. Goals should be objective and measurable (e.g., number of successful "up and downs"). Even a subjective experience, such as golf concentration, can be objectified to some degree (e.g., "On a 10-point scale of concentration, with 0 being complete distraction and 10 being 'in the zone,' I want to be at six or above on each hole of every round by midsummer").

Goal Setting, Slumps, and Burnout

Mark Calcavecchia

Several years ago I had a stretch where I could not have cared less. I made the mistake of playing some tournaments when I really didn't want to be there. Call it burnout, lack of interest, or whatever, but I was teeing it up in the morning and getting up there on the first tee and just swinging away at it. Sometimes the ball would go straight right or something, and I'm thinking, what kind of shot was that? Are you going to take this serious or what? I just couldn't get it together.

I think rest out here is important. You have to take your little breaks here and there to get yourself remotivated to come out and want to do well. Life on the tour can get to be one week after one week after one week. Sometimes you don't know where you're at. You wake up and think, *What tournament is this, anyway?*

Recently, I have set goals involving schedule management that help me avoid burnout. For one thing, I really do take the "off

season" off. I may go to Japan or Australia at the end of the year, but usually for only two weeks, and I play only up to the first week of December before heading home. Once I get home, I don't play at all for 20 to 25 days. I get a good break, and then I practice and play a little bit. I get limbered up before I go over to Hawaii for the first tournament of the year. Doing it this way, I am ready to go in January. Three weeks off—that's usually long enough for me.

For all golfers, from the novice (but serious) golfer to the elite professional player, goal setting is critical to getting any golf change off to a start that has a chance of success. Here are some important tips when setting goals for golf:

1. Begin with short-term goals that build to a longer term and bigger goal.

2. Make your goals specific, measurable, and observable.

3. Develop a method for measuring your progress on all subjective and not easily observable goals, such as motivation or anxiety control.

4. State goals in the positive: "I will use my focusing exercise on every green today" is better than "I will not let my thoughts stray at all today."

5. Self-monitor by keeping records of your goals, starting points, progress, and degree of success.

6. Never set goals that are incompatible with each other. For instance, don't set a goal to improve your chip shots when you have another goal to improve your anxiety level on the greens. If you do poorly toward the first goal, it will affect your second goal.

7. Never set goals where you can't understand exactly how to accomplish the goal. For example, don't set a goal to "stop being nervous during tee shots." Instead, set your goal "to perform my imaging and focusing exercise before every tee shot in today's round."

8. Never practice without at least one goal, even if the goal is nothing more than to have fun. Practice without a goal is low-grade, unfocused exercise.

The worksheet on page 10 will help you with your goal setting.

Understanding and Awareness

The second step in GUIDES is *understanding and awareness.* Golfers who are trying to accomplish their goals need a good understanding of where they are currently and an awareness of what is occurring as they practice a certain skill toward meeting a goal. Being able to understand the results of your conscious efforts is an important element of goal attainment. To acquire understanding and awareness, you will need to develop a mechanism for quantifying the target goal and identifying your current level of the goal behavior. Once this is done, you will be able to monitor your progress toward meeting a goal.

Monitoring Your Progress

As we've mentioned, once you have established a clear-cut goal, you'll need an understanding of where you are currently so that you can contrast your current level with your desired goal level. This makes it possible to monitor your progress. Sometimes understanding your current level is easy. Over a week, you can count how many times you hit the fairway or reached the green in three strokes. Other times, it is less easy to establish where you stand currently. If you're mis-hitting your long irons, for instance, and set a goal to resolve the problem, you will probably need an instructor to watch you as you hit long irons and give you feedback to base your specific goals

Figure 1.1 **GOAL SETTING WORKSHEET (EXAMPLE)**

1. Describe overall (large) goals. (Remember to make it as objective as possible and within a specified timeframe.)

Lower scoring average by 3 strokes within 3 months and maintain for at least 3 months.

2. Break down large goal into several subgoals. (Make objectives as specific as possible; specify timeframes.)

Long-term goal: *Lower average 3 strokes.*

Short-term subgoal A:

Increase number of greens in regulation by 2 in 2 months.

Short-term subgoal B:

Reduce number of putts per round by 2 in 1 month.

3. Quantify all subgoals and goals including subjective ones. Make up rating scale.

Rating Scales:

Subgoal A: 0–10 0=no success; 10=completely met goal
Subgoal B: 0–10 0=no success; 10=completely met goal

4. Decide on frequency of review of progress toward goal. After each month review progress.

5. Decide on reward/reinforcement for success at accomplishing subgoal and goal.

Long-term goal:	*The new woods I have wanted*
Subgoal A:	*The new wedges I have wanted*
Subgoal B:	*The new putter I have wanted*

upon. Obviously, a goal to "quit slicing my long irons" will get you nowhere!

Developing a method for self-recording your behaviors and progress is critical for meeting your goals. To help with this, we have developed a "peak performance record card" to increase your awareness of where you are and what's happening as you practice. The sample of this card, shown on pages 12 and 13, would help you monitor a round by a typical 10-handicap golfer.

The "peak performance round record" is useful for identifying golf problems through self-monitoring. In the example shown, you would use both the upper part of the card that helps you record the objective events of the round (e.g., where each shot went, where the putt was made from, and where shots were picked up or lost) and the lower part, which allows you to record important mental game changes hole by hole.

Implementation

Will Rogers used to say, "I will never be impressed by what you say you are going to do." Most efforts at change are like New Year's resolutions—well intended but never seriously pursued. One of the things most evident in our several years of helping golfers change has been their curious resistance to the first two steps in GUIDES. Because of this resistance, many golfers who say they want to change never even get to the third step, *implementation.* If you have done a good job on goal setting and increasing understanding and awareness, the implementation step is simple. During this step you decide which activities are necessary for you in order to acquire new golf skills or behaviors. In other words, you develop your plan of action. Generally, it's a good idea to write down this plan in very concrete, measurable terms, as shown in Figure 1.3 on page 14 in an implementation plan for improving your concentration on the course.

During this implementation stage, small changes will begin to occur in your thought, feeling, and behavior patterns. These changes will be stored and used while you're golfing. At first, the changes might be too small to recognize, but as additional changes occur they will eventually "add up" to a new skill. Once this skill has been acquired, it can be combined with another to produce a larger, more complete "mega-skill" that with further additions begins to take the shape of and function like the final

figure 1.2 PEAK PERFORMANCE ROUND RECORD (PRACTICE)

Name **BILL**　　　　Date _____　　　Type **REGULAR**

Hole	1	2	3	4	5	6	7	8	9
DRIVES									
Fairway	C	R		R		C	C		L
Bunker					S O			L	
Rough			R						
Water									
FAIRWAY SHOTS (PAR 5S)									
Fairway	L					R			
Bunker									
Rough									
Water									
APPROACH SHOTS									
Green	R	S O				L	L		R
Fairway	S O			S O			S O		
Bunker					L CP				
Rough			R CP		LO CP			L CP	
Water									
PUTTS									
L > 15 ft.	P 20	Bd30			Bd 25	Bd 20		P 50	Bd 30
M= 5-15 ft.		P 6	P 15	Bd 15			P 10	Bo 8	
S = < 5 ft.	Bo 3		Bo 2		D 4	P 4		D 2	P 4
GOOD SHOT: YES = 1 NO = 0									
1 or 0									
Course par	5	4	3	4	3	5	4	3	4
Your par	6	4	4	4	4	5	5	4	4
+/- Your par	0	0	0	-1	+1	0	-1	+1	0
CHECKS RATE: 0 = low, 5 = high									
Confidence	4	5	5	5	4	4	5	4	4
Health/Physical	4	4	4	4	4	4	4	4	4
Energy management	4	4	5	5	4	4	5	5	4
Concentration	3	3	4	4	5	5	5	5	5
Knowledge/Strategy	3	3	3	4	4	4	4	4	4
Pre-shot routine	4	4	5	5	4	4	4	4	4
Post-shot routine	4	4	5	5	4	3	3	3	4

Key Terms				CHECKS Rating 0-5	
C=center	Lo=long	E=eagle	Bo=bogey	0=none; very poor	3=high average
L=left	S=short	P=par	D=double bogey	1=poor	4=good (an asset)
R=right	Cp=chip	Bd=birdie		2=low average	5=great (very beneficial)

12

(continued)

Figure 1.2 *(continued)*

Hole	10	11	12	13	14	15	16	17	18
DRIVES									
Fairway	L								
Bunker			R						
Rough		L	L		R	L	R		R
Water									
FAIRWAY SHOTS (PAR 5S)									
Fairway	R								
Bunker									
Rough						R			R
Water									
APPROACH SHOTS									
Green	R	S O			LO			LO	LO
Fairway									S O
Bunker			R CP	R CP	L CP	L CP	C CP	R CP	LO CP
Rough				R CP					
Water									
PUTTS									
L > 15ft.	Bd15		P 15	P 20		Bd60	Bd40		
M=5-15ft.	P 5	Bd 15	P 5	Bo 8	P 10	P 15	P 8	Bo 12	P 10
S < 5ft.		P 3		D 1	Bo 3	Bo 3	Bo 1	D 1	Bo 2
GOOD SHOT: YES = 1 NO = 0									
1 or 0									
Course par	5	4	3	4	4	5	4	3	5
Your par	5	4	4	5	4	6	4	4	6
+/- Your par	0	0	0	+1	+1	0	+1	+1	0
CHECKS RATE: 0 = low, 5 = high									
Confidence	4	4	4	3	3	2	2	2	2
Health/Physical	4	3	3	3	2	2	2	2	2
Energy management	4	4	4	4	3	3	2	1	2
Concentration	4	4	4	4	3	2	1	1	2
Knowledge/Strategy	4	4	4	3	3	3	2	2	2
Pre-shot routine	4	3	3	3	2	2	2	1	1
Post-shot routine	4	3	3	3	1	1	0	0	1

Figure 1.3   IMPLEMENTATION WORKSHEET (EXAMPLE)

Goal (or subgoal): *Improve golf course concentration from an average of 3 and range of 1 to 5 to an average of 6 with range of 4 to 8 in 3 months.*

How:

1. *Practice relaxation exercises 2 times each day for 30 total minutes, 6 days per week for 3 months.*

2. *Practice attention/focusing exercises 4 times each day for 40 total minutes, 6 days per week for 3 months.*

3. *Practice "staying in present" exercises 4 times each day for 20 total minutes, 6 days per week for three months.*

4. *Monitor progress on 1-3 above using Peak Performance Record.*

5. *Reward 90% or better compliance each week.*

Reward: Daily: *Verbal self-reward (e.g., Good job today on concentration program)*
Weekly: *Deposit $1 per day toward vacation*
Monthly: *Dozen new Balatas or equivalent*
Goal Achieved: *New golf bag or equipment*

desired goal. Of course, before all of this occurs, you need to follow through with the fourth GUIDES step of regular and disciplined practice.

Disciplined Practice

Implementing the change program is part of the battle, but we all know how often we've started the process of making a change only to have it fade away as the newness of the exercise disappears and the grind of the day-to-day work on the project becomes tiresome and boring. Although the daily, weekly, and even monthly rewards for progress may help keep you motivated to carry out the project, it is the *disciplined practice* of the thoughts, feelings, or behaviors that over time gradually begin to look more like the desired goal behaviors. Psychologists call this process of triggering behavioral responses that resemble the target goal behavior "successive approximations of the goal," and the gradual change of the responses in the direction of the behavior we call "shaping." We gradually shape the swing or the putting stroke to look and feel more like the goal swing or putting stroke, and it is important, both for motivation and to demonstrate progress, to keep a practice record that allows for easily identifying progress and recognizing periods where no progress, or even backsliding, is occurring. This is where we move into *evaluation,* the fifth step in GUIDES.

Evaluation

Using a practice record helps you easily evaluate your progress toward your goal behavior. We have included on page 16 an example of a practice record kept during a golfer's anxiety-reduction program.

As you can see, there's nothing magical about the practice record form shown in Figure 1.4. Any type of form on which you can assess your progress and your compliance with your implementation plan will work fine for evaluation. The important point is that evaluative record keeping is necessary to keep a change program going.

Satisfaction and Reward

Finally, the last crucial step in the GUIDES is *satisfaction and reward.* Without adequate rewards for skills you accomplish as you progress toward your goal, all of the previous steps probably aren't enough to keep a change program going. Satisfying rewards should be built in at each phase of the change process, with an emphasis on rewarding implementation and regular disciplined practice. Even if you think that a step toward reaching your goal should be rewarding enough in itself, research on change clearly indicates the need for regularly rewarding your "subgoals" (the small steps toward the ultimate goal) to supplement the intrinsic rewards of improvement.

Rewards can be small or large, concrete or more abstract, personal or impersonal, and they are appropriate for every effort or outcome. The only limit to constructing adequate incentives and rewards for yourself is your own creativity, so use your imagination and come up with some new ways to treat yourself. I knew one golfer who rewarded himself by asking friends out to lunch. If he showed no progress, he had to eat alone that week!

Figure 1.4 **GOLF GOOD PRACTICE RECORD (EXAMPLE)**

Goal (or subgoal):   Anxiety Reduction

Month: _____

| | Days of Week | | | | | | | |
Weeks	Sun	Mon	Tues	Wed	Thurs	Fri	Sat	Reward
1	30	31	1	2	3	4	5	
2	6	7 D 4,4 M 5,4 I 5,4	8 D 6,7 M 6,6 I 5,4	9 D 5,4 M 6,5 I 6,5	10 D 5,5 M 5,5 I 7,6	11 D 4,5 M 5,4 I 5,4	12 D 4,2 M 4,2 I 5,5	YES
3	13	14 D 4,4 M 7,5 I 4,2	15 M 6,4	16 D 4,2 M 6,5 I 4,3	17 D 4,1 M 6,2 I 5,3	18 D 5,2 M 5,4 I 5,4	19 D 4,2	NO
4	20	21	22	23	24	25	26	
5	27	28	29	30	31	1	2	

Behaviors to Practice

1. D = Diaphragmatic breathing
2. M = Muscle relaxation exercise
3. I = Imagery relaxation exercise

Record Criteria: 1x/day ea.
6x/week
Anxiety Level:
Rating Scale: 0=10
    0 = Very relaxed;
    10 = Most anxious ever
    1st number = before practice
    2nd number = after practice

Taking It to the Course

All this theory is nice, but it's not useful unless you can see how to apply it, or "take it to the course." We'll now show you in detail one way we used the steps in GUIDES to help bring about change. We called the program the "Beck Growth Project." As we describe the program, we'll break down each step to show how it applied to Chip's unique situation.

Chip's Goals

Chip had a clear sense of his goals, so we had no problem organizing them into "golf-related goals" and "semigolf-related goals." Chip's specific goals were actually subgoals falling under a main objective of improving his scoring in PGA tournaments in general and, more specifically, improving his scoring in the major tournaments. It was clear that in the majors Chip was struggling with his tension level and confidence that he could, in fact, "get over the hump" and win his first major. In some of the other tournaments, Chip identified a different problem, which was maintaining a consistent level of good concentration, particularly when he had played many consecutive tournaments or when he was playing a tournament he didn't particularly enjoy.

Chip's other goals were to strengthen his ability to stay in the present and concentrate on the shot at hand, to avoid "thought regression" into the past and "thought progression" into the future, and to block out concerns, conflicts, or difficulties on and off the course so that they did not intrude into his focus and concentration and affect the immediate task at hand.

Chip's Understanding and Self-Awareness

I was surprised how well Chip understood where he was starting from and what he would need to do to reach the goals he had in mind. His emotional sensitivity and other personal characteristics indicated an extremely high "emotional intelligence," which resulted in little need to record his status or starting levels in several of the subgoals toward increasing awareness. However, like everyone else, Chip did benefit from the use of self-monitoring to help him see his progress toward the subgoals and the larger and broader golf and life goals.

I monitored Chip's progress myself as well, in two ways. First, we agreed that when he was at home in Illinois we would meet at my office, where he would report on his progress toward his goals both verbally and in written summaries. These reports would include his frequency of practice of the exercises that we had agreed on, as well as his feelings about how much he was benefiting from them. Our meetings also gave me the opportunity to evaluate Chip's presentation during our sessions. For some of his subgoals, I could evaluate his level of progress from that behavior sample. Second, Chip and I agreed that some of our work should be done at the tournaments he played, as we felt this would give us a chance to evaluate his efforts and progress and then adjust the programs and exercises as needed to make gains. Also, because we were going to be working toward several different goals, some more golf-related than others, we realized we needed a fairly specific game plan for our work together.

We decided to do the work that could be done off site (e.g., mental skills training) while Chip was at home, either between tournaments or during weeks when he chose not to play a tour event. We also agreed that some of the work would best be accomplished on site; I would attend his tournaments with him, including the three major tournaments held in the United States (the Masters, U.S. Open, and PGA Championship).

We felt that the three-part approach to our involvement—mental skills assistance at tournament sites, mental skills and personal consultation assistance at home, and joint projects—would be effective toward developing a strong business relationship that could significantly help Chip during this period of his career. Finally, Chip viewed this period of his life and career as a time of readjustment. He expected a temporary downturn in golf performance. He expected to go through some significant changes in his personal and family life. At the same time, he hoped to grow and develop new skills that would help him on and off the course, and in some other areas, such as public speaking. We were excited about the game plan and anxious to enter the implementation phase of our project.

Implementing Chip's Program for Change

We began by focusing on mental skills that are beneficial for optimal performance in sports. The main targets we chose were concentration, self-confidence, anxiety/arousal level, staying in the present, and shot routines. These would be our first orders of business and the ones we would primarily work on at tournament sites.

Before the first tournament Chip and I attended together, we had worked in the office for about six weeks. During that time we laid out much of the groundwork for the Beck Growth Project. In addition to extensive interviewing and taking a personality test, Chip completed a modified version of Thomas and Olders' Golf Mental Skills Assessment Questionnaire (1994). He tested above the 90th percentile on all of the scales we used, which indicated he had no significantly deficient areas in his mental skills for golf. Thus, our initial efforts in this area were to sharpen and focus his mental skills, to make them maximally beneficial for his upcoming tournament play. These efforts paid off with a third-place finish at the Nissan Open in Los Angeles. Chip shot seven under for a 277, good for a paycheck of $68,000.

Disciplined Practice Sessions

Two weeks later, at the Buick Invitational, we set a goal of having at least one mental skills "practice" session each day of the tournament on three selected mental skills areas. The first areas we chose were concentration, energy/arousal, and confidence. Thanks to Chip's recent third-place finish at the Nissan, the last area was the easiest.

It should come as no surprise that following a superlative outing in their sport, elite athletes generally have little problem with their confidence level. Chip's strong showing in the Nissan was energizing and rewarding, and it was a very simple matter for him to replay that recent tournament in his mind to reaffirm recognition of his talent level and his ability to perform at the highest level of his profession. Thus, in working on his confidence level, we engaged in one of the simplest forms of mental skills training—a replay of a recent positive experience in his imagination, recalling each stroke of his four rounds at the Nissan, visualizing his play on each hole. We focused particularly on the holes that resulted in his best shots—the birdies, successful up and downs, drives in the fairway, sand saves, and so on. We did this using a routine we came to use regularly at tournaments and in my office.

To enhance Chip's concentration, he imagined vividly in his mind's eye some of the best shots he had made during his morning practice round. He was also instructed to re-see as clearly as possible some specific objects and events he had come across earlier in the day. We practiced his ability to create "tunnel vision," where he practiced seeing his target line and target as the center of his field of vision. As he focused down the tunnel, he narrowed this field to include little more than these targets.

We also had Chip practice diaphragmatic breathing work (where your breathing originates more from your stomach than from your chest), which helps decrease arousal and energy level. Most professional athletes recognize the value of controlling their tension and energy and arousal levels. The ability to raise or lower this activity level is like manipulating the idle of an automobile engine. The routine requires focus and sensitivity, but it can work to anyone's advantage, especially during preparation for a specific performance. Chip spent 45 minutes practicing these routines. When he was done, he declared himself relaxed and focused; he felt ready to perform.

I had seen Chip perform the imaging and breathing exercises many times in my office, but I was impressed by his enthusiasm and ability to do them on the night before a big tournament. When he finished the mental work, Chip returned to his room for a physical workout. His physical routines combined well with his mental exercises and helped him sleep well before his rounds.

Evaluating Chip's Progress

What I saw the next day confirmed for me the value of my accompanying Chip on tour. Chip struggled throughout his round, ending up with a 73, which put him in a difficult position to make the cut the next day. As I followed Chip throughout his round, I observed him very closely. I watched his face, his expressions, and his body language. I even used binoculars to help me lip read some of his conversations with his caddie.

I saw no evidence in Chip of an emotional reaction to his struggle on the course that day. Although he had been playing well in recent tournaments, it was clear that Chip had "been there before," struggling through a round without letting it get to him emotionally. I saw no evidence of anger and very little frustration. I saw Chip attempting to solve his difficulties on the course. He looked like a professional going about his work on a day when it was indeed work! Despite the struggle, Chip appeared to be enjoying himself. It wasn't surprising to me at the end of the day, when we sat down to discuss the day's events, that Chip was still as upbeat and positive as he had been after our meeting the night before. He confirmed what I had observed during his round: he had done a good job of focusing on his many good shots of the day. Since he was sitting on 73, we both knew he was going to have a hard time making the cut the next day, but we never mentioned that. Instead, we prepared for Friday.

That night Chip did a mental skills routine similar to the one he'd done the night before, except this time he imaged replaying the good shots from the first round. Mistakes, bad breaks, and bad shots were not replayed.

It paid off with a better round Friday. Chip made fewer mistakes, got fewer bad breaks, and putted better than he had on Thursday. For a while we thought he might squeeze in under the cut, but he didn't get all the birdies he needed on the back nine and wound up with a round of 70.

To summarize Chip's round on Friday: he had started the day with high enthusiasm, energy, and concentration that wavered little as struggles appeared. When his scoring picked up during the middle of the round, his energy and enthusiasm also rose slightly. But some of the extra push diminished once he realized he was not going to make the cut.

Nowhere during the Friday round did I observe Chip lose his temper, behave rudely, or exhibit any of the behaviors sometimes seen from PGA tour golfers when things aren't going well for them. If I had been a teacher grading Chip's use of concentration, energy and emotion control, and confidence techniques, I would have given him a B+ at the start of his round. His mental skills execution increased to an A for many of the middle holes, and he settled back to a B+ as his chances of making the cut faded on the last three holes.

After the round on Friday, Chip signed his scorecard, practiced for two hours, and then went to work out. His desire to practice after missing the cut was one of the many examples of Chip's professionalism I would see over the coming months. That night over dinner he told me he'd decided to stay in La Jolla until Saturday night to give us all day Saturday to work together. He could have caught a flight right away, but he didn't.

Despite the disappointment of Chip's missing the cut, we learned and accomplished much at Tory Pines. Because of the extra work time on Saturday, we met or exceeded our goals for the week. We emphasized the positive, put the negative in perspective, and prepared to move ahead. I had accompanied Chip at only one tournament, but I could see already why he's known as one of the most positive players on tour.

Satisfaction and Rewards

After our work at Tory Pines, Chip and I rewarded ourselves for our efforts and progress we had made on our mental skills program. The reward part is important, and you can't neglect it. A program is much more likely to succeed if rewards for progress and work toward your goals are established and carried out. An external reward system always helps at the beginning of a change process, as it is in the beginning that it's most difficult to maintain difficult changes. New behaviors are fragile in the early stages, and anything you can do to maintain the changes will help. It's no big secret among psychologists that self-rewarding your changes, even when they are small, is the easiest and best way to help change continue as you move toward attaining your ultimate goal.

chapter 2

Preparing to Play

Preparation and Routines

Kenny Perry

I prepare the same way for every tournament. Obviously the majors are worth much more money, but I put lots of time into all my tournaments. Some guys might not prepare as much for Bayhill or the Houston Open as they would for Augusta, but to me they are *all* major tournaments, and I'm going to put 110% into preparing for them. I need to put in the time. I've been out here over 11 years, but I still feel that I need to put in two practice rounds and to get out and work the greens.

In my opinion, course management is everything. It's not how far you hit it. It's not how good your putt is. It's where you put it to give yourself an opportunity. That's what you have to do—give yourself opportunities to make it happen. Whether it's Augusta or Bayhill, I do the same thing week after week. I play practice rounds on Tuesday and pro ams on Wednesday. I always make sure to get a good feel for the greens. It's crucial for me to know what the greens are doing.

I notice that when I'm in the "zone," when I'm playing really good golf, I hear nothing. I hear no cars, no people, no nothing. I'm so focused, so tuned in, and it's so easy. But if I'm a little off sync, I'll back off until I can go into my routine. You sit out there and make a routine, and you approach each shot the same way. I approach the shot with conviction, with one shot. This is the shot I'm going to play. I'm going to stick with this shot and that's the shot I'm going to hit. And if I pull it off, great. If I don't, at least I'm not up over the ball and indecisive. At the last minute I'm not thinking, no, you need to turn it over and knock it down a little bit. You should never fight yourself over a golf shot. If I just stick with one shot, I'm okay. And if my concentration is off, that's when I go to my routine, when I sit and work on the practice range. I've got to start over. I back off, get regrouped, and just take my time and relax. I'll just relax and let my body relax. I relax and tell myself, "Try not to overhit the shot. Just execute. Trust your routine. Make the swing you've always made."

Make It Routine

If someone followed you around with a video camera all day and then played the tape back for you later, you'd see many examples of your unique behavioral routines. The first one might be your "getting out of bed" routine. The particular way you swing one leg and then the other over the side of the bed and step down, walk to the bathroom and push the door open, flick the light switch, and look into the mirror and rub your eyes. All of these movements you might repeat daily in nearly the exact same way. You've done them so often that you don't even think about them. If you question how automatic these habits have become, replay in your head all the movements you use to perform a common routine such as brushing your teeth. This "simple" task actually consists of many complex maneuvers, all of which you do automatically. If you thought about each movement as you performed it, the movement as well as the task would become self-conscious, less natural, and probably less efficient.

KEY PRINCIPLE: DEVELOP A ROUTINE

Building good shot and other preparation routines for golf is the single most effective technique to improve your game. Good routines are the essence of performance consistency. Carefully constructed routines that incorporate your practice experience, past positive playing experience, and preparation to play will lead to consistently better scoring.

Routines are sets of behaviors organized into steps toward performing complex actions. A pre-round or pre-shot routine consists of small behaviors (some thoughts, some movements) sequentially organized to move you toward your goal—in this case playing the tournament or hitting a shot. The primary purpose of the routine is to make a goal easier to accomplish.

Gradually, the repetitive execution of the step-by-step behaviors within a routine "melt" into a smooth and fluid execution of a larger behavior. This new behavior is a composite of the many smaller ones smoothed out, melted together, and made largely automatic. As an example, think of the first time you drove a car with a manual transmission. Recall the difficulty you first had in organizing and coordinating the sequence of behaviors necessary to work the clutch, the gas pedal, and the gearshift. In the beginning you had to think your way through this complicated series of movements, and for a while the end result probably made for a jerky ride full of abrupt stops and starts. However, as your nervous system began to combine the individual smaller behaviors into a composite, larger one, you were able to drive the car more smoothly. As your new skill developed over days and weeks, your nervous system continued to combine your hand and foot movements into a coordinated sequence that ultimately resulted in your ability to drive with ease and confidence.

If you want to see how routine and automatic driving a "stick" has become for you, the next time you're driving in a safe place, try to think your way through all the movements involved in working the clutch, the gas pedal, and the gearshift. Tell yourself what you are going to do next *before* you do it. Notice how rough and uncoordinated your movements become. You're back to that jerky ride you started with before your movements turned automatic.

Good golf preparation routines "set up" your nervous system to carry out the behaviors desired. Routines alert your nervous system that you want to do something very specific, and they prepare your mind and body to carry out the familiar thoughts and actions. Thus, good preparation routines lead to both consistency and familiarity. They are also critical for concentration and blocking out negatives. Because routines allow you to perform complex sequences of many behaviors without thinking, you're able to focus your attention on just a few critical triggering thoughts, movements, or even sensations, greatly simplifying execution of the task. And if your mind is engaged in carrying out a sequence of frequently repeated mental activities, it is much more likely to stay on track and not be deterred by negative thoughts or worries breaking in to knock your thoughts off-course or contaminate them with performance-affecting negative activity.

One of the most important aspects of developing routines is that with regular practice they do, in fact, become automatic and somewhat unconscious. The *overlearning* of your routines is what makes them automatic. We gave an example earlier of brushing your teeth and how automatic that routine has become for most of us. Driving to work is a similar automatic routine. Sometimes you get so engrossed in your thoughts that you don't see the streets you're passing or notice the turns you take. You suddenly find yourself at your destination without remembering how you got there. Sometimes this worries people. They think, if I can't remember the turns I took or the things I passed, I must not have been aware—I could have hit something. But they *were* aware. If during the drive there had been a need to avoid an accident, that too would have happened automatically.

It's of great benefit for golfers to develop a pre-round preparation routine, a pre-shot preparation routine, and even a post-shot and post-round review routine that will "kick in" and carry them through automatically. Because routines alert your nervous system to initiate a desired sequenced behavior, you can focus on one key aspect of the situation at hand, such as correct torso movement during your swing. Developing routines can significantly elevate your level of play.

PRESCRIPTION FOR DEVELOPING ROUTINES

- Organize your mental and physical preparation activities into an easy-to-remember acronym
- Develop post-play routines to help you benefit from the shot itself and get maximum learning from the round played

Organizing Your Routine

In the talks and workshops we've given over the years, we've recognized that golfers and other athletes benefit most from mental skill techniques when they can "crystallize" them into a simple set of skills—a routine—that they can easily remember. The routine should include the main elements of mental *and* physical preparation, and it should be able to become automatic and carried out without much thought. Out of the many labels for pre-performance activities, we picked the easy-to-remember acronym CHECKS, which includes the first letter of the most important mental and physical skills to combine into a pre-performance activity or routine. The CHECKS are *confidence* and the mental and behavioral skills that produce and maintain it; *health* and the routines necessary to maintain a readiness to perform; *emotion and energy control* and the activities necessary to develop and maintain this control; *concentration* and its component skills; *knowledge* including play experience; and *strategies* including game plan and routines, the organizing and sequencing of the physical and mental preparation activities into pre-performance patterns that lead to consistently high levels of performance.

The CHECKS should be organized into a practice routine that allows for the consistent repetition of the necessary skills. The routine should also serve as a diagnostic tool which, when carried out, identifies one or more of the CHECKS that might be deficient. Once an area is identified as lacking, the golfer is in a good position to "step up" practice activities to bolster the deficient skill area.

There are several advantages to organizing your mental and physical preparation activities into a routine such as CHECKS. A routine will make it easier to

- practice your confidence-building exercises,
- carry out your physical activities to prepare your body for play,
- check your emotional control and energy level,
- check your level of concentration,
- review your knowledge base for the tournament, and
- review how well you have combined these activities into pre-tournament and pre-shot strategies to prepare yourself to hit the individual shot you want or to play the course the way you want for the entire tournament.

We've seen many instances of players with good intentions preparing for play. However, in their anxiousness to get started, or in the heat of battle, they fail to do their intended preparation activities. Many golfers use the CHECKS system, or a similar one, to go through the preparation activities one at a time, identifying those that are deficient, bringing them up to proper performance levels, and then "checking them off" before proceeding to the next CHECK. We have found it is easy to do this in preparation for a round or tournament, and even in preparation for individual shots. We do want to emphasize that we don't believe there's anything inherently better about our particular ordering of preparation activities into CHECKS, except that the acronym makes it easier to remember the steps. Some golfers might prefer a different ordering of the steps, something like CSEHKC, and if they can remember the steps that way, more power to them!

Pre-Tournament Routine

Chip Beck

I like to arrive at a PGA tournament by late Monday afternoon, and if I can get some chipping and putting in, I feel that's a good starting point for the week. It removes the feel from the previous week and

gets me ready for a fresh set of greens. I start by getting a "read" on the greens—how much they break and which way. I'll usually try a few long putts to get a feel for the speed of the greens. Next, I chip around the greens to get acquainted with the different rough and pin placements. If I can start chipping on Monday afternoon, I consider that a bonus.

On Monday night I start preparing my body

physically. I do push-ups, sit-ups, and my stretching routine. Sometimes my body fights the stretching, especially if I've had a couple of weeks off, but I know that I need to keep limber, so I always finish the routine.

On Tuesday, I like to play a practice round, by myself if possible, so that I can chip and putt and go at my own pace. I also usually practice an area of my game that should prove helpful for the week, whether it be a wedge from 60 to 70 yards in, just driving the ball, or maybe hitting some medium to long irons. Then, on the course, I like to continue my preparation by doing some chipping around the greens and doing a lot of putting from different pin positions. Finally, I practice my short game for as long as I can around each green without holding up play.

Sometimes I'll play just 9 holes and spend a lot of time chipping and rolling the ball around the greens and hitting all kinds of sand shots, seven iron chips, or any kind of imaginable chip shot that might be necessary that week. Often you can tell by the size of the green and the depth of the bunkers what chip shots will be required. If the bunkers are deep, I'll practice getting the ball up quickly to make sure I can get it up out of the bunker. I make sure my technique is good and that the club face is opening up. I check aspects of my swing that apply to bunker play. If the grass is soft or the soil muddy, the club face might be slowed down significantly, so I try to get a feel for the different types of grasses. For instance, in Florida, where most of the grass is pretty tough (Bermuda grass is very difficult to deal with), a certain style shot is often required, and I'll try to figure out what's best for getting up and down from 10 feet.

I'm most effective when I practice short game work that requires significant concentration. While practicing the mechanical parts of my game, I'll also spend considerable time "seeing" the ball go in the hole. This helps my confidence and gets me mentally prepared for the days ahead.

Although I may vary my pre-tournament routine a little each time, it always contains these same basic ingredients. If I tried skipping the routine, I'd feel that something was missing or that the week hadn't begun properly.

Post-Play Routines

CHECKS is an excellent routine to practice before a round and individual shots, but post-play review routines are also quite useful. To maximally benefit from each shot, you should develop a *post-shot* routine in which you evaluate the decisions and movements that preceded the shot and occurred during the shot. Similarly, you should develop a *post-round* routine to get maximum learning and benefit from the round just played.

A post-shot routine should include a quick evaluation to determine whether you can learn anything positive from the shot. There's always something positive to get out of a shot that we like, a shot that closely resembles the one we had envisioned in our pre-shot routine. If the shot matched well with that pre-shot routine image, it probably had a positive outcome (unless it hit a sprinkler head!), and it is deserving of a positive reward for yourself. The reward will alert your nervous system that what just took place is worthy of storing in your memory for replay.

If the shot only roughly approximates the imaged shot, or has only components of the imagined shot and others quite different and considerably less desirable than the imagined shot, you should replay, and reward, only the positive parts of the execution and ignore the others. If the shot in no way resembles the imagined shot, a quick review of the shot might reveal what went wrong. If so, there is something to learn from the shot and this insight should be stored. If the review yields no information about what went wrong, it's best to put the shot behind you and forget you ever hit it.

If you do your post-shot reviews during the round, you should later be able to replay the round stroke-by-stroke in your imagination. This is your post-round routine, and it should include only the positive elements from the round—those successful shots that matched their pre-shot images and the *parts* of other shots that were performed as you intended, even if the shot itself fell short of your desires.

Using CHECKS as Your Pre-Round Routine

In developing their pre-round routines for preparation, PGA Tour players will invest more time and energy than what we're suggesting here, but the routine we'll describe is realistic in terms of the amount of time and investment that an average player can make in preparing to play golf. This abbreviated routine might be used by a nonprofessional golfer who enjoys the game a great deal and wants to play it as well as possible.

As you develop CHECKS as your pre-round routine, you need to decide where, when, and how often you're going to practice the steps. In the beginning, having a specific place and time, and even a specific pattern of practice, will make it more likely that the practice will occur. At the start, each practice session should include no more than two or three CHECKS at a time, and you should try to dedicate at least 20 minutes to each. If you spend at least 40 minutes a day, this means you'd work on at least two of the CHECKS daily, resulting in each step getting attention twice per week. Expect to have difficulty with at least one or two of the steps, and it's to these you'll want to devote more time and energy (without neglecting the others).

We'll now summarize each of the CHECKS steps and briefly explain how it can bolster your game.

BECK'S CHECKS

Confidence

Health

Emotion and energy control

Concentration

Knowledge

Strategy

We have included a worksheet for your pre-round preparation routine on page 33.

Confidence

Confidence is a belief in your own capacities and a reliance on your own abilities. For an aspiring golfer, self-confidence can be seen as a complex of internal events based on a healthy ego and positive self-concept. This base is bolstered by supporting positive input including past successes, positive feedback from others, positive reviews (self-evaluations or others' evaluations of you), positive

Figure 2.1 PRE-ROUND PREPARATION ROUTINE

Tournament _____

Date _____

Preparation components: **CHECKS**

C = Confidence
H = Health/physical
E = Energy/emotion
C = Concentration
K = Knowledge/game plan
S = Strategy

Day	M	TU	W	TH	F	SA	SU
Confidence							
Health/physical							
Energy/emotion							
Concentration							
Knowledge/ game plan							
Strategy							

Check carried out? Yes =√; No = ×

Reward criteria: 5 of 6 **CHECKS** carried out today? _____

6 of 7 days during tournament week? _____

self-statements concerning value and worth, and positive self-images. The last two refer to both performance-related and non-performance-related self- statements and self-images. Since confidence is derived from both positive personality traits *and* a positive history of experience and regular positive feedback, your confidence can be bolstered through the practice of mental exercises that are gradually absorbed into and adopted by your psyche. As these practices are absorbed and adopted, your self-concept and basic ego structure are transformed.

One of the first things serious golfers should do is attend to their level of confidence. If you work on your confidence early, you'll be more ready to progress through the other CHECKS steps with enthusiasm.

Most people think that the more confidence they have, the better—but, in fact, sometimes confidence levels are too high for optimal performance. More often the opposite is true (that confidence is too low), but you should go into your confidence check with a clear mind, open to the possibility that you may actually need to work on *lowering* your confidence level.

Once your current level of confidence has been identified (see chapter 3), you need to choose activities either to raise or lower the level to match the reality of your preparation and of actual competition. Practiced frequently enough, confidence-altering exercises will affect your precompetition confidence level more quickly than you might think.

Health

You need to check your level of health, or physical preparedness, to make sure you're physically ready to perform. We won't go into physical preparation here, as there are hundreds of books out there to tell you how to physically prepare for your chosen activity. The main point is that you need to work *within your routine* on your ability to assess your current state of physical readiness. Building this step into your routine will keep you attuned to the slight variations in your body (e.g., mild stiffness or soreness) that might require a modification in the other steps of your routine or in your performance. For instance, if a minor pinched nerve in your back is bothering you, you will probably need to adapt your concentration level to overcome the distraction. This step is the time to check for anything out of the ordinary your body might be telling you. It might be as minor as a mild hunger (eat a granola bar) or as major as a chest pain (see a doctor), but whatever it is, you'll need to take care of it before you proceed to step three.

Emotion and Energy Control

Your *emotion and energy control* involves your state of autonomic, neural, emotional, and cognitive activity. What does this mean? It means you might be anxious, nervous, excited, angry, depressed, lethargic, relaxed—or some of these plus others all at once. Emotion and energy control involves your emotional state, your thoughts and feelings, and your physiological activity (such as your heart rate, blood pressure, and muscle tension). It is influenced by both your inherited predispositions and your learning history. For instance, you might be predisposed by your genetics to exaggerated emotional responses to stress. Or your past experiences (your learning history) might make you respond in a certain way to a poor shot or a round's worth of bad breaks.

For most golfers, an intermediate level of internal activity, or emotion, is best for performance. In rare cases, a golfer might thrive on a high level of emotion, while another might perform better when unusually subdued, but as a rule you want to keep an even keel.

Techniques used for lowering your energy level include diaphragmatic breathing exercises, imagery, positive and calming self-statements, progressive muscle relaxation, and hypnosis. Several of these techniques reduce emotional reactivity and improve impulse control, while elevating mood and improving confidence and concentration. Techniques used for raising your energy level include "pumping up" through "chest" or "backward" breathing exercises, competitive imaging and self-statements, and progressive muscle tensing.

Once you have assessed your emotion level, you can modify it fairly easily through the techniques just mentioned (also see chapter 4). You will want to get your emotion level to its optimal state before you progress to the next step.

Concentration

In our context, to *concentrate* means to exclude all other incoming stimuli, focus your attention on your target, and develop your target line so you can execute your mechanics effortlessly, without thought. Like confidence and emotion level, concentration can be too low to permit optimal performance or too high to be sustained through 18 holes of golf.

Concentration can be disrupted in many ways. In some cases, it is influenced by negative thoughts or images that intrude into your consciousness. In other cases, it is affected by unusual success or an emotion level that is too high. Low or poorly directed concentration can interfere with performance by complicating your stimulus "picture," making it difficult to focus on the truly important stimuli involved in execution. Low concentration can result in losing track of your performance or game plan, possibly leading to a neglect of important information such as course knowledge or changes in wind speed or direction.

One way to improve low concentration is through self-observation and carrying an ongoing dialogue with yourself. Talking to yourself about the task at hand helps you identify when you have become distracted and allows you to refocus on what is important to maintain good performance.

The main problem with concentration being too high is that it can be extremely fatiguing; it may be impossible for you to maintain high concentration over a whole round of golf. Sometimes it works to "turn down" your level of concentration when you are in between strokes, as this conserves your energy for your pre-shot routine, shot execution, and post-shot routine.

For more on improving your concentration level, see chapter 5.

Routines, Confidence, and Concentration

Mike Reid

I believe very strongly in a pre-shot routine. I think that's a real key to consistency. If you're making a routine approach to the ball, I think your brain knows when to hit it. I think if your approach is erratic and inconsistent, your game is going to be that way as well, because your brain never quite knows when the ball is going to be struck.

Someone who had watched Nicklaus en route to winning the 1986 Masters told me that it had taken Nicklaus exactly 13 seconds from the time his club came out of his bag until he hit the shot. It was rarely 12 seconds, and it was rarely 14. Nicklaus is a type A personality, granted, but I think even golfers who aren't type A—guys like Trevino and Lanny Watkins, who stand up and just hit it— if you watch their routine, it's the same thing every time. Their routine is their signature, and they own it.

I think you have to find something in your pre-shot routine to help you focus in on the shot. This gives your brain a chance to know when you're going to hit the ball. It should be pretty much the same every time. A good pre-shot routine gives you one less thing to think about on the course.

Sometimes sloppy habits work their way into your pre-shot routine. When this happens, I think you can usually find a wealth of things that you've gotten away from. They're not just physical things you do, although these can be very important and can throw off your game, but also psychological. Your thinking can get askew. Sometimes you're not concentrating on the right things in the right order, and that can throw you off. I remember I was in a slump one time because I was taking three looks at the target instead of two. When I looked at what I was doing, I found that my first look was general, my second look was specific and my third look was general again. I played poorly for a whole month because of that extra look. Once I went back to looking only twice, my game came back just like that. I know that sounds hard to believe, but I was comfortable with two looks, not three.

Confidence and concentration are vital parts of the pre-shot routine. I started golf when I was four or five years old, and the joy I had was the feeling of a well-hit shot coming off the club face, the way the grass smelled, and the way the ball bounced when it hit and rolled on the green or up near the hole. I wasn't capable of saying to myself, *left arm straight, head down.* I didn't really know much of what that meant. My dad started me on the game very simply and worked on only a few fundamentals. At that age, you're not capable of remembering a great deal, but you are capable of seeing it in 3-D before you hit it.

Unfortunately, you can get away from that as you get older, and then you have to relearn how to do that. How to stand behind the ball and see what it looks like in the air, what it feels like coming off the face, and what it looks like bouncing on the green and rolling close to the hole.

That's the essence of concentration. And, to me, confidence is encapsulated in the effort. And it *is* effort! It is a mental muscle up there. Visualization is closely tied to confidence, and I think if you can see your shot, you can hit it. And some shots, whether on driving ranges, in different wind directions, no matter what you're working on, if you can't see it, it is going to be very difficult to hit it properly. You can stand out there until you're blue in the face with 100 balls, but until you can stand back behind it and say, "Yeah, that's what it looks like it ought to do" and get comfortable with that, you're never going to hit it right. Once you can do that, though, confidence and concentration suddenly aren't an issue. You're golfing the shot, and all that crap that commentators say about this being the most important shot of your life becomes irrelevant because it isn't the most important shot in your life—it's the only shot. It's just as important as the first shot you hit that day or the last shot. Your mind ought to be thinking about what it looks like, feels like, and, for auditory learners, what it sounds like. If you're into that, then all of a sudden confidence and concentration aren't issues any more. It's just a matter of following that image, and as Chuck Hogan taught me, you're re-creating something you've already seen. You truly get what you think.

I know that physically and mechanically I've gotten about as far as I'm going to go. Any improvement I'm going to make now is going to be from the shoulders up. It didn't take a great revelation for me to figure that out. Once you get to the level where you understand the concepts of the swing and what makes it go well enough, what you need to work on is between your ears.

Knowledge

Reviewing your *knowledge,* or your experience base, is the fifth step of your CHECKS routine. This review includes drawing on your playing experience, the importance of the tournament you're playing, the type and level of competition you have, and a review of how you've been playing to help set expectations. You should review important aspects of the course, the factors needed for shot selection and construction, and the performance cues you have chosen for this particular outing. It is also during this step that you might choose to review the goals and subgoals you've chosen for the competition ahead and the ways in which you hope to accomplish them. This review should help you to focus on what's most important, and in this regard, it will help your concentration as well.

Strategy

The last step of your CHECKS preparation routine involves several run-throughs, or rehearsals, of specific *strategies* that you use regularly. If you're an experienced golfer, you should have several strategies or routines to run through that you perform in any competition before every stroke, whether it be a drive, an approach, or a putt.

The better and more consistently you can perform the six steps of your CHECKS preparation routine, the more ready you'll be to handle any course or competition that you come up against. No matter how talented you are, and no matter how much you practice, there's absolutely nothing more important to success than good preparation. We have outlined the critical steps to take toward good preparation. In the section that follows we'll show you in more detail how to apply a complete shot routine that includes preparation as well as performance of the shot.

Taking It to the Course

A good shot routine should include abbreviated elements of some of the CHECKS along with activities that set you up to swing the golf club, using everything at your disposal to make your shot the shot you have imagined it should be. We have developed a seven-step pre-shot routine that will give you an advantage over many opponents who don't use it. This routine should help you execute a high percentage of your desired shots.

The Seven-Step Pre-Shot Routine

Our seven-step pre-shot routine builds upon a routine that Chip has developed over his many years on the tour. We have added two components to capitalize on what behavioral scientists know about preparation and performance and about how the body works in terms of performance. At the end of the chapter, we have included a figure showing our seven-step pre-shot routine to make it easy for you to follow along with our description of its steps, their purpose, and how to most effectively use them.

Your shot actually begins as you approach the ball. Whether the ball is in the tee box, on the fairway, or on the green, as you approach it your body and mind should begin a sequence of activities that essentially builds a shot for you. The shot that is built should be easy to execute because it will be a combination of your natural talent, your swing practice, your "play history," your mental attitude and overall mental game at the moment, your analysis of the shot to be hit, and the conditions of the moment (conditions include both internal conditions such as fatigue level, and external conditions such as the weather conditions and your place on the leader board).

Step 1: Breathe to Control Tension

As you approach the ball, start adjusting your energy and tension level. Usually this involves systematic breathing to take your arousal down a notch, as most players get excited or nervous in anticipation of hitting the ball. If you play "flat" (i.e., your arousal level is low), and you find it difficult to get up for the shot or the round, then the first step in your routine will also involve breathing, but it will be a pattern of breathing that arouses you physiologically rather than relaxes you. The relaxing pattern of breathing, called *diaphragmatic breathing*, involves extending your abdomen as you inhale, and then contracting your abdominal muscles as if you're blowing up a balloon, as you exhale. (We describe these breathing patterns in detail in chapter 4.) A few deep diaphragmatic breaths calm you at this very important stage of your shot. They also signal your nervous system that what's coming is a familiar and frequently practiced sequence of mental and physical actions that your nervous system has blended over time into one long "megaresponse." It's very important to cue your body in this way to alert it to what's coming next, particularly when what's coming is familiar and practiced.

Remember that if you play flat (with low arousal), you'll want to pump up your body at this time instead of relaxing it. In this case, another breathing pattern, often called "backward" or "chest" breathing, should occur at the beginning of your shot routine. In this pattern, you inhale by expanding your chest and exhale by letting your chest and stomach contract, similar to "chest out, stomach in" while standing at attention in the military. A few pump-up "reps" done this way will push adrenaline into your system, raise your heart rate, contract your muscles, and make you feel a little stronger momentarily. Unless you're one who is too tense off the tee, a few pump-up reps when particularly flat or when trying to get a few extra yards will work to your advantage.

Step 2: Analyze the Situation

While your body is physically changing in response to the diaphragmatic or pump-up breathing pattern, it's time for your brain—more specifically, your left brain—to enter your shot routine. It's at this point that you want to construct the shot you want to hit. The process includes focusing on the external conditions affecting the shot, including the distance, the wind, the lie, and your place on the course and in the tournament. It also includes identifying your internal conditions—your energy level or fatigue, confidence level, concentration level, and anxiety level.

Step 3: Assess the Shot

At this point the left side of your brain—the analytic, logical, and organizing side—attempts to find information in its "playing history database," looking for answers to the questions, "Do I know this shot? Is this shot familiar?" and "Can I hit this shot?" If your brain can answer these questions in the affirmative, it then brings up out of the database a "copy" of the shot that you intend to hit. This is not unlike accessing a file in your computer.

If, however, your brain does not find "yes" answers to these questions, you will have to construct a shot—that is, you'll need to piece a shot together using a problem-solving process. In this process you sort through various ways that the shot could be made before selecting one that you think *and* feel will work best, considering all the factors.

Step 4: Image the Shot

You want the left side of your brain to do only one more thing before it shuts down and gets out of the way for the rest of the shot. You want it to transfer its information to the right side of your brain, the part that's responsible for emotion and physical performance and which thinks primarily in pictures or images instead of in words. In as much detail as you can, you want to create a mental picture of the shot to be hit.

A major variable in this process is that some players choose to make the left-to-right brain transfer and subsequent creation of the mental picture of the shot before executing their practice swing, while others prefer doing it after their practice swing. You should try it both ways to see what works best for you.

It's at this point in your shot routine that some of the real magic happens, as it's here that your brain is capable of doing several amazing things. The image of the shot that has been created—a shot you have practiced many times on the practice tee and hit possibly many other times during your playing career—gets accessed from the practice and playing experience database and is made available to you through your formation of the shot image. Then your brain takes this copy of previous successes executing the desired shot and transfers the information to the muscles of your body needed to carry it out.

What you have done is program your body to execute the shot that you planned to hit. This has occurred through bringing into the present past examples of having hit the shot successfully. If you have no successful images of hitting the shot in your brain's database, then you have created a shot in your mind's eye, you have imagined hitting that shot successfully, and you have included in the image the positive outcome. In this latter instance, you have in effect given your nervous system a successful execution of the desired shot to work with in its preparation for hitting the shot, even though you have never hit the shot before!

Step 5: Feel the Shot

The next mental action is even more amazing. The right side of your brain transfers the necessary information to the muscles of your body needed for execution of the shot, along with messages for carrying the shot out. This step is a drawn-out description of what is known as "feeling the shot." The picture or image of your shot has become a kinesthetic and sensory one, and your body is preparing to hit the shot that you have presented it with.

Step 6: Execute the Shot

Some golfers trigger this execution with a "swing thought" and others with a cue to focus on some body position or sensation. The process begins with attending to how your body feels as you execute the stroke, including your follow-through, and comparing it against both the shot that you imagined and the sensations that your body has given you during your many swings on the practice tee and on other shots. Here you're looking for a close match between what you have just done and what you've practiced and imagined doing. If the match is very close, you have likely hit the shot that you want, and if so, it is a shot that you'll want to remember and "store" both physically and mentally.

Step 7: Review the Shot

Did the ball follow your desired and imagined target line? If you hit the shot you wanted but did not hit the target line you probably did not set up properly and were not aligned in such a way that the correct shot execution would send the ball along the desired target line.

By focusing on where the ball landed and finished, you're in position to know whether you accurately constructed the shot regarding club selection, external factors or forces, and the amount of energy invested in the shot. You're also in position to evaluate your mental condition during the shot and how closely you followed your seven-step shot routine.

At each point in the post-shot evaluation process, you want to notice what you did well, store what you did well, and reinforce yourself for having done it well. You also want to notice what you didn't do well, attempt to determine what went wrong and store that information, and then dismiss all negative parts of the shot, never to be thought of again.

The evaluation of the quality of the shot compared with the practiced and the ideal; the evaluation of the set-up and the ability of that set-up to result in the desired shot execution, including putting the ball on the target line; the evaluation of the correctness of the constructed shot (the game plan for this particular shot); and an evaluation of the execution of the pre-shot routine—all of this evaluating is nearly as important as the pre-shot routine itself in terms of its potential benefit for improving your performance.

Between shots in your round, during that "downtime" following the post-shot routine and prior to the next pre-shot routine, recover your energy and perform an abbreviated version of the CHECKS to assess how you're doing in terms of confidence, emotion and energy control, and concentration and how well you're sticking to or using your game plan and shot routines. A quick review of how you're doing on the CHECKS also alerts you to when you need to give yourself a booster of one or more of them, or, said another way, to keep them more in mind as you continue to play your round.

We've included sample worksheets for the pre-shot and post-shot routines, shown on pages 45 and 46.

Figure 2.2 SEVEN-STEP PRE-SHOT ROUTINE

Tournament _____

Date _____

Steps:

      1. Use deep, diaphragmatic breathing.

      2. Analyze the golf situation.

      3. Is the shot familiar?

      4. Image the shot.

      5. Feel the shot.

      6. Execute the shot.

      7. Review/replay the shot.

Day	M	TU	W	TH	F	SA	SU
1. Deep breathing							
2. Analyze							
3. Familiar?							
4. Image it							
5. Feel it							
6. Execute it							
7. Review/ replay it							

Criteria: Step carried out?   Yes =√;   No = ×

Reward criteria: 6 of 7 **CHECKS** carried out daily on 6 of 7 playing days? _____

figure 2.3 FOUR-STEP POST-SHOT ROUTINE

Tournament _____

Date _____

Steps:

1. Evaluate the shot (compare the actual against imagined).
2. Review set-up.
3. Review correctness of constructed shot.
4. Review the execution of the pre-shot routine and
   mental condition during the shot.

Day	M	TU	W	TH	F	SA	SU
1. Evaluate shot							
2. Review set-up							
3. Correctness of shot							
4. Review routine; mental							

Criteria: Step carried out on 90% of shots?   Yes =√;   No = ×

Reward criteria: 3 of 4 steps carried out daily on 6 of 7 playing days? _____

chapter

3

Believing in Your Game

Confidence, Not Arrogance

Tiger Woods

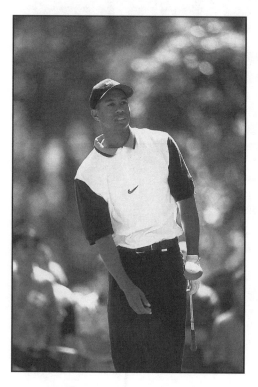

Not since Jack Nicklaus has there been someone with the potential to completely dominate the game of golf. In the first 21 events of his professional career, Tiger Woods never missed a cut and won six tour events, including the Masters. Nicklaus has predicted that if Woods stays healthy and confident, he will win 100 tournaments and 20 majors over the course of his career.

Like Jack Nicklaus, Tiger Woods is confident. He's not arrogant, he's confident. He's *so* confident that it frightens some other players who know that confidence breeds success when you have the game to back it up. After the 1997 Western Open, when asked if he was surprised at his play and his success at such an early age on the Tour, Tiger replied, "I'm not surprised. If I play my normal game I should be able to win out here on tour. . . . I think the biggest thing is to have the mindset and the belief that you can win every tournament. Nicklaus had it. Every time he'd tee it up, he felt he was going to beat everybody." Here is Tiger, at 21, mentioning himself in the same breath as Jack Nicklaus and to himself probably feeling like he will be better than Jack—the Michael Jordan of golf. Tiger wants it to happen, he expects it to happen, and guess what? It's happening.

Confidence Skills

While we all experience crises in our lives, we don't often think about crises in confidence. We may not even recognize that we're going through one. Confidence, like self-esteem and attitude, is a nebulous concept that we seldom try to define—we just wish we had more of it. We attribute many of our poor performances to a low level of confidence. We might know we have the strokes, the skills, the stamina, and the heart, but none of these matter much when confidence is low. What many people forget is that confidence, too, is a type of skill that can be learned, practiced, strengthened, and applied. If you build up a strong enough confidence base, it will come through for you even in times of crisis.

KEY PRINCIPLE: SELF-CONFIDENCE

Self-confidence is a set of learned thoughts, feelings, and actions that can be acquired by anyone, not just a lucky few who seem to always have it. Confidence must be practiced, just as you practice your swing, and when it's practiced frequently, confidence becomes a habit.

People who are rarely confident (you know who you are) do have some different thoughts and feelings from those who are confident almost all the time, and you also do some things differently than they do. Psychologists have studied the thoughts, feelings, and behaviors of the confident and compared them with those of the less confident. The differences are striking. One of the biggest differences is in the type of thoughts these two kinds of people think. Confident people think confident thoughts that include "I can" instead of "I can't" and "I will" instead of "I won't." For the confident, the focus is on succeeding rather than on failing. Their thoughts involve expectations of success. Their thoughts concern potential gains, not losses, and they regard the pluses about the issue or task at hand rather than the minuses. The confident golfer might say, "I will make this putt," not "I hope I don't miss it." Actually, the confident *smart* golfer would be more likely to say, "I'll make my stroke smoothly through the ball and make the ball roll smoothly with the right speed and directly on my line to the hole," because the confident smart golfer focuses on execution rather than on outcome.

Another general rule is that confident people *expect* success as opposed to hoping for it. When success occurs, they accept it as the inevitable outcome of their effort, desire, practiced skills, and preparation. If you're a confident golfer, because you expect success, you likely regard difficult shots or holes as challenges rather than obstacles or enemies. Challenges excite you rather than elicit fear, and you move in the direction of challenge. As a confident golfer, you look forward to the difficult holes or shots as opportunities to learn and grow, as chances to stretch your skills and raise your game to a higher level. Finally, although confident golfers are not afraid of taking risks and may take a few more risks than unconfident golfers, confidence is not about risk taking per se, as confident golfers are patient and wait for real opportunities on the golf course. They are confident there will be another opportunity, perhaps a better one than what they have at the moment. One example of this is when Chip Beck "laid up" at the 1993 Masters. On the famous par 5 at Augusta, Chip knew he would be decreasing his chances of catching Bernard Langer by attempting to hit a perfect shot under less than perfect conditions. He was confident he could birdie the hole after laying up, and then birdie the remaining holes, and very likely force the tie and a playoff. He was confident he could play one hole at a time and make up the difference by doing so. This is not unlike a basketball team that is behind by 20 points in the beginning of the fourth quarter and concentrating on catching up one basket at a time.

The Masters Lay-Up

Chip Beck

My decision to "lay up" on the 15th at Augusta National on that Sunday in 1993 came after much consideration. First and foremost, I felt that I was playing really well. I knew where the pins were on 17 and 18, and I felt that I could birdie those holes. Even 16 was a good pin for me. I felt that on 15 the most important thing was to give myself the best opportunity to make a birdie. I needed to take the risk out of the hole to ensure that I could make birdie and give myself a chance to play the last two holes, even if I were two down with two to go. I felt if I could birdie the last two, I might be in position to win my first Masters in a playoff.

That was my plan. I wanted to be in position after that hole to play the tournament out. I was far enough down at that point (three strokes behind Bernard Langer) that I needed a birdie to give myself a chance. As I approached the shot, I was about 10 yards farther back than I had practiced from with a new wood I was playing that week. I had hit two shots with a similar (though not quite as strong) wind as was blowing on Sunday. I had hit it well, but I couldn't clear the water. It wasn't a matter of lacking confidence. I knew there was no question I was going to hit a good shot. It was just a matter of positioning myself. Also, I would have to put the ball up in the air because I was in between two mounds of the fairway. I couldn't keep the ball low and out of the wind.

It was a tough decision for me, but I knew that even if I hit a perfect golf shot, I could come up short in the water. That would be throwing away with one shot any chance I had of winning the tournament. I felt that was not the strategy to take to win the golf tournament. I felt the better decision was to lay up to the left so that I had a good shot into the pin. That was my strategy, and that's what I went with. I was hitting on all cylinders, and it was just a matter of getting myself the best chance to play all the holes out. I thought that was the best way I could win the Masters.

There is *always* something positive in a round of golf to feel good about, even if it's only one shot out of the whole day. Confident golfers replay that one shot, dismissing the others, and tell themselves, over and over again, that that one shot is an example of what they can and will do on better days.

It is true that some people just seem more confident than others, and these people seem to have been confident all their lives. Confidence probably is inherited to some degree, as more and more of our basic personality traits are being recognized as at least partly genetic. Still, confidence is more a practiced skill than an inherited trait, and it is certainly a characteristic that can be enhanced in anyone. But it does take practice.

Practicing Confidence

Confidence, just like your golf swing or your putting stroke, must be practiced. We don't ordinarily think of practicing our thoughts, and confidence *is* largely a matter of what thoughts we're thinking. If your thought is *I know I'm a good golfer,* and you have this thought frequently, you're much more likely to become a good golfer than if you think you're no good at the game. And through practice you can improve the thoughts you think about yourself.

The key element of practice is the repetition of specific and clear steps or thoughts. For instance, in reference to the statement *I know I am a good golfer,* it would be important to repeat this exact statement perhaps 50 times a day if you want it to register. As any advertising agent will tell you, repetition is the key to remembering.

Low self-confidence works the same way. People with low self-confidence routinely tell themselves how ineffective and useless they are. They focus on how often they fail, and naturally that is the information registered in their mind. Unfortunately, it is dangerously easy to turn "I have failed" into "I am a failure." For building confidence in golf, it's important to regularly think and act like a golfer who has more self-confidence. If you're low on confidence, this means practicing confidence-building thoughts and confidence-building actions on a regular basis. You need to practice good confidence habits as frequently as you practice driving, chipping, and putting.

Positive Reinforcements

Hale Irwin

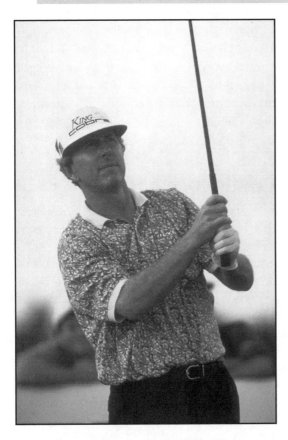

I was nearing 40, and I didn't know how much more of this I wanted to do, traveling and playing. It was getting really old, so I set up a golf course design company, and the efforts that had been going into playing golf now were split, 50% to golf and 50% to this other venture. Well, 50% is not enough to play successfully out here. You might be able to set up a business and hire people to do a lot of it, but that wouldn't work here. I played for four years just horribly and ended up with little to show for it. The years 1986 through 1989 were terrible years, and that was coming off a win here in 1985 (the Memorial), so it wasn't like it was three or four years later.

At the end of 1989, I sat down, took out a legal pad, and wrote down all the tournaments I had won. I wrote down my thoughts and remarks, going back to my first win. I wrote down everything I could remember. This started a positive reinforcement process. It got me thinking back to what I used to do, to what I was and wasn't doing now, and I realized that I was thinking differently.

This period in my life got me back on a game plan that had worked for me for a long, long time. I had gotten away from it, not so much because of my design work, but I had just let things drift away. So, my win at the Open in 1990 and the subsequent win at Westchester were not surprising to me, though I think to the golfing world, it was. But I knew I could do it. I just had to go back and find the formula again. I had to go back to what was natural and instinctive for me, and to understand me again. That took a little while to filter in, but I could feel it coming. After four years away, it doesn't come back overnight. It took time, but it came back a little each week. Gradually, I played with more and more confidence, and that has continued on to where we sit today. Confidence is a building process.

Making Confidence a Habit

It's important to remember that when practiced frequently enough, confidence becomes a habit, just like practice builds other habits, such as regular exercise. We do develop many positive mental habits such as the mental steps we go through in solving a problem. Because the habit of thinking from A to B to C and finally to D has been so practiced and "grooved in" we don't consciously have to think of that sequence when solving a problem in our schoolwork or in our business activities.

We have many negative mental habits such as obsessing, particularly on the negative, and most of us have at least some of the more minor characteristics of people diagnosed with obsessive/compulsive disorder. The tendencies to obsess and worry are very easy for most people. At times it seems easier to establish negative thinking patterns than positive ones, just as it seems easier to develop bad habits than good ones. Think of how often you worry about something and have difficulty putting the worry out of your mind. Many people believe golf is the most difficult sport, mentally, because golfers have so much time between shots to worry and obsess over the negative.

Benefits of Confidence

There are many benefits of confidence that directly apply to golf. First, confidence increases your energy level, so the more confident you are, the more enthusiastic and excited you can get about your play. On days when your confidence is higher, you'll have more energy on the course, walk faster, and make quicker decisions, and your decisions will likely be more effective. When you're depressed, you have low energy. When you lack confidence, your energy level is quickly sapped. As your confidence improves through self-confidence exercises, you'll see indisputable gains in energy and enthusiasm, for both golf and life.

Confidence also improves concentration. It brings mental sharpness, mental efficiency, and an improved ability to focus. As you work on boosting your confidence, your imaging abilities and your focus will likely improve; your chances of finding that "zone" you always hear about but never experience will increase. You can't make the zone happen for you, but if you prepare to play in all the ways we're suggesting in this book, you will have done all that you can to set the circumstances for it to happen to you.

BENEFITS OF CONFIDENCE

- Increases motivation, enthusiasm, and energy level
- Improves concentration and sharpens mental skills
- Makes experiencing the "zone" more likely
- Decreases your fear of taking risks
- Shrinks the tendency to catastrophize
- Increases adherence to practice routines
- Improves self-discipline and reduces procrastination
- Produces a relaxed and focused state of mind and body and reduces tension
- Reduces slumps and the tendency to choke

A high level of confidence increases your willingness to take reasonable risks when making shot selections and developing course strategy. The key words here are *reasonable risks,* as confidence doesn't make you reckless or daring to a fault; big egos, bad judgment, and poor impulse control do that. What confidence does is increase your willingness to take a chance when you have adequately prepared for the task. You'll be more likely to "go for it" when it's truly a good opportunity. Confidence also helps shrink your tendency to "catastrophize" (i.e., to see a failure as a disaster or the beginning of your demise). Rather, you see a failure for what it is—simply one event that was not a success in your life.

At the professional level, confidence allows tour players to play good golf because, without it, they would not survive the inevitable four or five bad shots they make each round. And at all levels, confidence increases compliance with practice routines. When you lose your confidence and are discouraged, your motivation for doing work, particularly hard work, suffers. You may feel, *what's the point?* Confidence gives you the faith that your hard work will pay off, and it's the sense that there will be a payoff from practice that keeps us practicing and performing the routines frequently enough to ingrain them and make them a part of us.

As you practice the confidence-building exercises and notice your confidence increasing, you'll see that you're more disciplined, that you behave more responsibly in regard to playing golf, and you'll find, almost paradoxically, that you feel good and more free about playing the game. Most of us feel good about positive routines, dedicating ourselves to positive efforts, and doing hard work. Finally, believe it or not, most humans *do not* like procrastinating. Each of us knows people who get all their tasks done quickly and early compared to others. Most of us envy them because we see that they seem freed up and happy not to have the tasks hanging over their heads. Confidence will help you manage your time better. You'll no longer put things off out of fear of failing or because they seem too much to take on.

Yet another benefit of confidence is that it produces a relaxed and focused state of mind and body. Confidence directly combats both the mental and physical anxiety we call "tension." Because increased confidence helps you relax, it directly improves your ability to execute the golf swing and focus on execution. Finally, confidence reduces slumping and choking (topics we'll discuss more in chapter 6). Lack of confidence is often to blame for a slump getting started, and it makes it harder to break out of a slump. Although choking is usually caused by interruptions in concentration and execution routine, confidence also plays a role, as concentration contamination and disruption occur less often in confident players.

CONFIDENCE PRESCRIPTION

- Believe in your preparation
- Remember your successes
- Expect to succeed

Believing in Yourself

It seems nearly every year some baseball, football, or basketball team hits on a slogan that it rides to success. "The Pack is Back." "Three-Peat Repeat." "You Gotta Believe." All slogans help inspire a team, but this last one in particular sums up our first principle for building confidence: you *gotta* believe in your skills, in your game, and in yourself. If you don't, you may as well store your clubs now.

Throughout history it has been demonstrated that humans can do amazing things when they believe in a cause and have faith they can do it. But it's not as easy or as simple as it sounds to believe in yourself. In fact, several players on tour have told me the largest hurdle they had to overcome was to get to the point that they truly believed they could succeed at the professional level. A lot goes into cultivating a belief in yourself. For one thing, you need a reason to believe in your skills and your game. Before you really have anything to believe in, your natural golf skills must be developed and your game constructed. The skills that make up your game develop only when you have effectively practiced and adequately prepared yourself to play. Thus, you must learn to trust your preparation. *Belief* and *trust* are important words in golf. Unless you learn to trust your preparation, you can't have confidence and play well.

If there is any such thing as an "equalizer" of athletes, it is preparation. Only preparation can give athletes with less natural talent a chance to truly compete with the most gifted athletes of their sport. Learning to trust that your preparation can give you an edge is critical to building confidence and taking advantage of what confidence can do for you.

Remember Your Successes

Jack Nicklaus has won more than 70 professional tournaments, but he also has many other golf awards and achievements to draw on when he wants to take advantage of past successes (dubbed "Player of the Century" in 1988; PGA Player of the Year in 1967, '72, '73, '75, and '76; U.S. Amateur champion in 1959 and 1961; NCAA champion in 1961; 18 international titles). Most of us, however, are less like Jack Nicklaus and more like tour players who have never won a tournament. We have to draw on significantly lesser successes in golf to build our confidence. Fortunately, though, we don't have to limit ourselves to our golf successes in order to contribute to our confidence building. If you have had success in your job, in physical activities or sports other than golf, or in your home raising your children, you can re-live these success experiences and let them contribute to your overall feeling of self-worth and self-confidence. Also, remember that your nervous system doesn't discriminate between a recent win and a win several years ago. Either can help raise confidence.

Expect Success

Nothing builds the confidence to expect success as much as successful execution of what you are trying to accomplish. And as we've said already, it doesn't matter too much to your nervous system whether you actually execute the action or *imagine* executing it. To rehearse in your mind the shot you want to hit is a form of practice, and it's one that contributes to the actual creation of the desired shot. Thus, rehearsing the shot you want to hit in detailed imagination not only contributes to making the shot but increases the chances that the shot can be hit, and it also increases the confidence that the shot will be hit at least on occasion in the beginning and more frequently later on. Chip Beck and most other tour golfers regularly imagine the shot that they want to hit. They do this during their pre-shot routine, when they are practicing, and many other times during the day.

Staying Confident and Playing Loose

Lee Janzen

I think confidence is the most valuable skill anyone can have. Anyone who is extremely confident is going to be tough to beat. They may not even realize that they have a mechanical flaw or something, and they can still win. Certainly other things are needed, but I try to recognize if I'm tentative over a shot or if there's a shot I don't feel comfortable about. When this happens, I try to make an adjustment in my confidence level right away. What helps me is that I try and give myself a double dose of confidence. I get more aggressive with my swing. I've got to be as passionate with this golf swing as I possibly can. I focus in on a spot and really zero in on the shot. I've noticed in the past that when I get tentative I tend to just swing at it and

really don't give it much. It's very hard to hit a good shot when you're doing that. You have to go out expecting to do well, and then if you can have that sort of confident, cocky, passionate attitude before every shot, then you'll get better pictures (images), you'll focus in on a better spot, and your mind will help your body perform better, too. Before I play every round I go through a little checklist of questions. The first one every day is, "What's great about today?" I want to be excited about today, every day. It could be raining and windy, just the ugliest day you've every seen, but you can always find a couple of great things about the day. Maybe it's a challenge ahead of you, or you've got to shoot a good score to make the cut or to get the lead. There's *always* something to be excited about. And sometimes when I'm not playing well, I just remind myself of my accomplishments up to this point, and you can go on and on. You can list anything. How many tournaments you've won, how many years you've been on tour, what place you're on the career money list, how many cuts you've made. And you should always remind yourself of any time you thought your back was against the wall and you pulled through or when you accomplished something that you thought you never could do. You should always remind yourself that there was a time when you weren't confident, and you still did it. You've really got to pat yourself on the back as often as you can—a lot more than you probably do.

How to Build Confidence

Confidence is a learned skill that must be practiced to become habit. The exercises in this section are designed to build your confidence by improving your ability to believe, trust, expect success, carry out your preparation program for successful shot making, and benefit from past positive experiences. The exercises include self-talk and imagery drills as well as desensitization and dismissing techniques, all of which have been tried with great success by many golfers. You'll need to experiment to discover which exercises work best for you, but be sure to give each of them a good honest try (over several weeks) before giving up on it.

Self-Talk Drills

Okay, so it can feel a little silly to repeat statements over and over to yourself, but we're here to tell you that the silliness wears off pretty quickly. Once you start to feel results, the self-talk mantras become like any other routine in your day. It also might help to know that some of the most successful athletes in all sports use self-talk to boost their confidence and get them going.

I know I am a good golfer. I feel good about my golf game. My game gets better and better the more I practice. These phrases, and ones similar to them, if repeated over and over on a regular basis, will gradually register in your brain. They will become part of your thinking. They will come to mind without your purposely saying them. And at some point they will become a part of you and contribute to your self-confidence. *I trust my preparation, my talents, and myself on the golf course. . . . I'm confident that I'm more prepared to play golf than I've ever been. . . . I trust my practice, effort, and dedication to pay off for me on the golf course.* In self-talk exercises you want to decide on one or two statements to repeat for each of the areas you wish to focus on. Commit to a program of repeating the statements over and over to yourself on a regular basis. With regular repetition, rehearsal, and practice of such statements, you'll find that you begin to miss them when you don't do them, to feel something's not quite right. When this happens, you'll know that self-talk has become a successful routine for you, and that's it's working to build your confidence and faith in yourself. Trust us; it will happen.

Imagery Exercises

You use imagery exercises, or mental pictures, to produce similar results to what you get from self-talk drills. Mentally "seeing" yourself practice, seeing your practice result in improvement, and seeing that improvement carried over onto the golf course will build your belief in your skills, your practice, and your game. Just as you should take time choosing and constructing your self-talk sentences and drills, take time to decide which images you like, feel good about, or even get excited about.

Imagery and self-talk techniques are probably the most effective methods of practice for programming in successful shot making. Frequent repetition of images of going through a powerful and effective shot routine, the execution of a perfect set-up and swing, and images of a perfect follow-through and result, will "groove in" the imagined activities and contribute to the building of confidence.

Imagery is the key for building what we call your "positive experiences history" or your "database" of positive experiences. These are golf- and nongolf-related imagery routines that help increase your confidence. Make a list of your successes and, for each one, write down as much detail as you can remember about the positive experience so that you can replay it in your mind in pictures as vividly, as three-dimensionally, and as virtually real as possible. As with self-talk, repetition is the key to confidence bolstering when using your positive experiences history or database.

Desensitization Techniques

Desensitization, a technique developed by psychologists to reduce or eliminate fears or phobias in people impaired by these problems, involves the pairing of anxiety-producing thoughts or images with a well-developed relaxation response, so that the relaxation response interferes with the negative thoughts or images producing anxiety and fear. For golfers who tense up at the mere thought or sight of water or an otherwise troublesome hole up ahead, desensitization can be used to remove, reduce, or eliminate the fear response that contributes to lower confidence and poor play.

List on paper a series of anxiety-producing events that could happen to you on the golf course. Now, beginning with the least anxiety-producing event and ending with the most anxiety-producing event, imagine each event occurring, slowly and in detail, as you remain relaxed. If you do this exercise regularly, then when you're on the course in similar situations to the ones you've repeated in your mind, your nervous system will be cued to kick in a relaxation mechanism, and you'll feel anxiety draining away. Regularly imagining the troublesome course situation, poor play, or other confidence-decreasing problems that can occur on the golf course, while successfully remaining in a state of relaxation, gradually reduces the ability of these troublesome scenes, thoughts, or events to produce anxiety and erode confidence.

Dismissing Techniques

Dismissing techniques involve using a repetitive gesture or image to, in effect, delete, throw away, or let go of a poor shot, bad decision, or bad hole. For instance, you might practice imagining crumpling the score card of a poor round and tossing it into the trash and walking away. Or you might imagine turning your back on a hole and never looking back, or waving good-bye to a bad hole and seeing it disappear in the distance. Or you might practice a hand gesture, such as a flick of the wrist, to symbolize a rejection of and dismissal of a poor shot or hole.

These techniques for gaining control over your mental game combine to increase confidence, and increasing confidence improves performance. For the techniques to work, they must be thoughtfully constructed and practiced regularly and frequently. Mental control and confidence-building techniques are equally important to preparation as your time on the practice tee and putting green. If confidence-building mental practice is not a large part of your preparation for play, you'll have a hard time competing against those golfers who do practice these routines. Mental toughness is a huge part of golf.

To make your use of these confidence-building techniques easier and more systematic, and to increase your likelihood of practicing them regularly enough for them to be effective, we have included worksheets to help you develop your practice program. The first worksheet includes instructions for developing your positive experiences history and how to use it in pre-play practice of past successes in golf and nongolf activities. The second worksheet is a multipurpose one that allows you to construct either imagery or self-talk drills for increasing beliefs, trust, expectations, and for successful shot-making mental practice. The third worksheet is designed to assist you in setting up a desensitization program for some troublesome aspect of your game and for its elimination through regular desensitization practice. Finally, the fourth worksheet is for dismissal practice. It's designed to help you commit to using dismissal techniques frequently and consistently enough to benefit from them.

figure 3.1 PLAYING WITH CONFIDENCE WORKSHEET

Key principle or skill: *Building a positive experiences history*

Method:
1. *Our positive experience is our total experience with a task or issue minus negative experiences with it. It can be stored (deposited) within us to be accessed or drawn upon to benefit our performance.*

2. *Positive experience deposits can be made by:*
   a. *Actual play that results in positive performance and success*
   b. *Actual play that is not successful but that results in the identification of solvable problems*
   c. *Imagined replay of (a) above*
   d. *Imagined simulations of the successful performances of others, with you playing their part*
   e. *Imagined replay of positive experience unrelated to golf (i.e., wedding day; winning an award)*
   f. *Imagined simulations of experiences unrelated to golf, with you in the action*
   g. *Positive self-talk*
   h. *The storage of (a) through (g) internally into an accessible working mental and muscular memory that combines with our skill repertoire to produce positive performance*

3. *Negative experience can be removed by:*
   a. *Desensitization techniques that reduce the impact and "staying power" of negative experiences*
   b. *Dismissal techniques that reduce negative experiences and their impact on us*

(continued)

figure 3.1 *(continued)*

Procedure:

1. *List positive experiences.*

   _____

   _____

   _____

   _____

   _____

2. *Practice/replay experience for* _____
   (length of time)

   for _____.
   (number of sessions)

3. *Record change in positive feelings/thoughts.*
   Scale = 0-10   0 = skill absent   10 = highest

4. *Rewards:* _____   _____
   Type   *Criteria*

   Practice sessions and change

	1	2	3	4	5	6	7	8
Before session								
After session								

figure 3.2 **PLAYING WITH CONFIDENCE WORKSHEET**

Key principle or skill: *Building belief trust expectation and*
shot-making

Method: 1. *Make list of images or statements to boost*
                confidence through repetition.
          2. *Reward practice, and progress.*
          3. *Reward progress.*

Procedure:

1. *List images or self-talk statements.*

_____

_____

_____

_____

_____

2. *Practice images or self-talk statements for* _____
                                               (length of time)

   for _____.
           (number of sessions)

3. *Record change in positive feelings/thoughts.*
      Scale = 0-10   *0 = skill absent*   *10 = highest*

4. *Rewards:* _____   _____
                     Type   *Criteria*

Practice sessions and change

	1	2	3	4	5	6	7	8
Before session								
After session								

Figure 3.3 **PLAYING WITH CONFIDENCE WORKSHEET**

Key principle or skill: *Desensitization for fears, trouble,*
or poor play

Method:
1. *Make list of scenes and images of fear, worries, negative thoughts, trouble on course.*
2. *Practice relaxation exercise(s) to develop strong relaxation response.*
3. *Pair problematic scene or image with relaxed state.*
4. *Reward practice and progress.*
5. *Reward progress.*

Procedure:
1. *List problematic scenes or images.*

_____

_____

_____

_____

_____

2. *Practice pairing scenes or images with relaxed state for*

_____ *for* _____ .
   (length of time)   *(number of sessions)*

3. *Record desensitization change (e.g. fear reduction).*
Scale = 0 -10   *0 = skill absent*   *10 = highest*

4. *Rewards:* _____   _____
           Type   *Criteria*

Practice sessions and change

      1   *2*   *3*   *4*   *5*   *6*   *7*   *8*

Before session

After session

Figure 3.4 PLAYING WITH CONFIDENCE WORKSHEET

Key principle or skill: *Dismissal technique development*

Method:

    1. *Decide on dismissal images, statements, or behaviors (gestures).*

    2. *Practice using above on negative thoughts, feelings, or actions.*

    3. *Reward practice and progress.*

    4. *Reward progress.*

Procedure:

1. *Decide on dismissal images, statements, or behavior.*

_____

_____

_____

_____

_____

2. *Practice dismissal techniques for* _____ *for*
                                         (length of time)

  _____.

  (number of sessions)

3. *Record change in ability to dismiss the negative.*

    Scale = 0 - 10   *0 = skill absent*   *10 = highest*

4. *Rewards:* _____

                      Type   *Criteria*

Practice sessions and change

	1	2	3	4	5	6	7	8
Before session								
After session								

Controlling the
Mental Game

The "TPC Experience": An Emotional Boost

Chip Beck

When I need an emotional boost or want to motivate myself to push harder or endure a difficult period, I replay my TPC Experience in my head. I close my eyes and imagine that I'm back at the TPC. It's 1989, and I am tied for the lead. On that day I was off to a really poor start. After driving the ball onto the fairway off the first tee, I pulled a four-iron to the left of the green. It was a windy day, I didn't get up and down, and it seemed to go downhill from there. I shot 42 on the front side and at the turn I had tears in my eyes. I felt so down about what had happened and how I had just let things go. I was playing under duress at the time with a lot of things happening on the outside. At the turn, I realized that I was far out of it, yet with a good second nine anything was possible.

At that point, I just said to myself, "Well, I'm going to pretend that I just had a great front nine." I was going to try to change the psychology of it because everything had been wrong. As I went to the 10th hole, I played it fairly well to the green, and I had about a 10- or 15-footer downhill. At that point, I really didn't have any confidence that I could make the putt, so I "pretended" that I just had made one before and thought, "Oh, wow, isn't that great?" I told myself it did happen and I felt like if I could just see this one go in, then it was possible that it could happen. So, I played the "made-up" good putt in my head and then played this one going in as well. Sure enough, I made the putt—and it was a really key putt.

I was playing with Tom Kite at the time, and I don't think he realized that I could be a threat that he was going to have to deal with on the back nine, after I had basically thrown the tournament away on the front. As I played the last few holes, I would have never dreamed that it would come down to sinking a birdie on the last hole for a chance to win. I made an incredible putt from about 25 or 30 feet for birdie, and Tom Kite felt like I was going to make it. He then had to make a good two-putt from the front of the green to win the tournament. He did, and it was a very good win for him.

For me, I felt as if my run at the end to finish second was like a victory because of the disappointment I overcame to go from a 42 to a 32. I think that was really phenomenal. I was proud of that moment

because I was able to change how I felt. I think that was one of the things I really have learned in the last five or six years—that if you can overcome disappointment, you can accomplish great things. Today I still replay this experience in my head to help me stay in a competitive frame of mind.

It's very difficult when you're disappointed or emotionally down to play golf. I would say it's impossible. It's a stroke of luck if it happens. If you can realize that you're not out of it until the end, even though it looks as if you've blown the tournament with three holes to go; if you can change the feeling and psychology of it a little bit rather than letting the discouragement and disappointment fill your mind and destroy your game, then you have a great opportunity to finish well and possibly even to win.

If you love your work and approach both the opportunities and the difficulties of your day in a loving manner, the challenges that you encounter will make you stronger. You may not always get the result you want, but you'll be satisfied that you did your best. I think that kind of satisfaction is what ultimate success comes from. You have to be satisfied that you did a good job and that you loved the challenge as you went along. Aristotle said that happiness is working for it, and I think that's true. The journey is the happy part.

Mental Magic

Unfortunately in golf, it's easy for a player to lose control mentally and either start slumps or keep them going. In some cases, such as in Chip's experience at the TPC, you can overcome a slump in the making through using your mental powers. But sometimes, no matter how hard you try to concentrate, you just can't seem to gain control of your game. When mental control collapses, players will find themselves having trouble with both the key principles we'll cover in this chapter: (1) controlling anxiety and anger and (2) achieving optimal arousal.

KEY PRINCIPLE: CONTROLLING ANXIETY AND ANGER

Successful golf depends on controlling anxiety, anger, and other strong negative responses that are a combination of both emotion and thought.

Although at first glance anger and anxiety seem very different, and most people can easily tell the difference between being anxious or being angry, our nervous systems don't really make that much of a distinction. Both are strong emotional reactions, both trigger physiological arousal and our "fight or flight" response, and both can seriously disrupt our golf games. However, the two are significantly different in that they consist of distinct thoughts playing in our heads, and they produce usually far different behavioral tendencies.

When anxious we may become quiet or start babbling incessantly or we may withdraw or run away. When anxiety is the most severe it can paralyze us and we're unable to do anything. Anger, on the other hand, often triggers more proactive responses, both in our heads and in our actions, at least for some people. However, other people respond to anger in a similar way that they do to anxiety; they become quiet, withdraw, and hold their anger inside. Incidentally, people who do these things and do not discharge their anger somehow but instead hold it in often get negative emotions like depression, or physical problems such as psychosomatic symptoms (e.g., headaches, other pain problems, digestive disorders, high blood pressure, skin problems). Somewhat surprisingly, research has demonstrated that unresolved or unprocessed anger is probably even more destructive for us than high anxiety, and, despite their similar physical elements, somewhat different techniques are needed for controlling anxiety and anger. We'll discuss these later.

We have all seen examples of the negative consequences of losing control of our emotions on the golf course. Although several tour players are known to have hurt their potential and their careers because of poor emotional control, there have also been many shining examples of tour players enduring the greatest kind of disappointment and frustration and overcoming it with grace and dignity. Remember Hubie Green standing over a four-foot putt to win the Masters, disrupted by the yell of a cameraman, his concentration broken by the unfortunate disruption, and his missing the putt and losing the tournament? How did he react? Probably no one would have blamed him if he'd blown up and cursed the cameraman. But he kept his cool, and I think he won many admirers that day. Another example of a player overcoming an event was Jeff Sluman, about to put away a TPC victory when, on the 72nd hole, a spectator screamed and jumped into the lake next to the hole just as Jeff was getting ready to finish. Disrupted and shaken, Jeff missed the putt and eventually lost the tournament, but he didn't lose his head as many would have in that situation.

Here were two players who had a right to be plenty upset and angry about their misfortune, yet they dismissed it and went on with their careers like the true professionals and champions that they are. Their emotional control skills, perhaps better than their concentration skills were at the time of these incidents, have helped them to have long and successful careers on the PGA tour.

You Can't Be Perfect

To play good golf, you need to control obsessiveness and perfectionism. Golfers, particularly those who take the game seriously, are very likely to take most of their other life activities seriously and in fact may be somewhat obsessive-compulsive or perfectionistic. Until fairly recently, golf was played mostly by well-off and successful people, and affluence and success often go hand-in-hand with achievement orientation on the positive side and obsessive-compulsiveness and perfectionism on the negative side. Most successful people know that they are obsessive at least to some degree and often perfectionistic. Some see these traits as faults to be reduced if not overcome, and others see no problem with them whatsoever. The latter group sometimes end up seeing clinical psychologists because the people around them are troubled by the person's obsessiveness or perfectionism, and the person has been told to get help for these problems "or else."

A tour golfer has to expect four or five bad shots per round. Those of us who are not tour golfers or who are not scratch golfers have to expect more than that number. But it's quite difficult for perfectionists to accept even one bad shot, let alone 10 or 12 or even 20. While the perfectionist struggles with the number of bad shots, the obsessive personality may have only one bad shot and be unable to put it out of mind. When one bad shot can't be forgotten, more bad shots usually result. Also, there seem to be some people who play golf who are not obsessive-compulsive and perfectionistic in any other area of their lives except their golf. We will talk more about golf's strangely compelling nature in a later chapter, but for now it's enough to say that golf makes some people obsessive-compulsive. Our techniques for reducing this negative quality will help keep this from happening to you and keep it from interfering with your ability to develop a better and more satisfying golf game.

Forget the Bad Rounds

Mark Calcavecchia

Sometimes bad shots on holes bring me down, sometimes I'm too hard on myself, and sometimes I can't forget about a bogey or double. Then I'll bogey the next hole, and I'll get mad because I let that bother me, and then sometimes I'm just flat out miserable the whole day. I wish I was better at that, but I'm not. I'm getting better at it, but sometimes I just have days where I really feel miserable the whole day, and I can't shake it. However, there's nobody that can forget a bad

round faster than me. It's really ironic that I can spend five hours out on the golf course feeling miserable, and then the second I'm in my car and leaving the parking lot, I'm fine. It's done. I can forget it and say, "Man, that stunk. What a lousy day." I hated it, but then as soon as it's done with, it's like, "Thank God, it's over," and then I feel better instantly. So, sometimes I wish I could use the way I am when I leave the golf course while I'm still out there, that I could bring that attitude a little bit more with me on the course in certain instances. This doesn't always happen to me, obviously, because you can't be a good player if you're out there messed up all the time, but I know I'm messed up *some* of the time.

Understand Attribution

Attribution is a very important term in psychology, sport psychology, and athletics, as it relates to *perceived cause and effect*. When something occurs it's natural to want to understand why it occurred, and we're most comfortable when we can look around and identify the cause of the event, good or bad. We use the words "perceived cause and effect," because often it doesn't really matter what the *real* cause of an event is; if we perceive that one thing causes another, events follow that are quite similar, if not identical, to what would happen if the perceived cause was indeed accurate. If a player comes to perceive that his driver is a primary cause of poor performance, and if he can't find a driver that works to improve his game off the tee, poor play is likely to continue, at least in part because of the perception that the poor play is caused by the driver. In this situation, poor play is likely to continue, at least until a perceived better driver is found.

If you look back at the last sentence and say, "Wait a minute! If the poor play thought to be caused by the driver really had little to do with the driver, then why would getting a better driver result in improved play?" You're right to question this. Changes in perceived causes of events do *not* result in changes in those events except for a short period of time where something else psychologists call a "placebo effect" often takes place.

A placebo effect is a situation in which something improves because we changed something that we believed would help the problem. Placebo effects are one of the reasons people try making all kinds of changes to solve their problems. When the problem improves for a short time, people are reinforced for making the change. This results in their continuing to do the thing that they believe helped, even long after the placebo effect has worn off and the problem has returned.

These interesting circumstances are what produce in many athletes a collection of unusual, sometimes weird, behaviors that they repeatedly do in a ritualistic manner. Often these behaviors can be seen just prior to shooting a free throw, coming up to the plate in baseball, or between innings in a clubhouse. (A Chicago Cubs pitcher recently seen brushing his teeth between innings comes to mind.)

Chip crossed a bridge on the road to "recovery" from his current playing slump when he recognized that it was probably inaccurate to attribute driving problems solely to the several drivers he had tried. This resulted in his seeking out another opinion as to possible cause, and as so often happens, someone else sees something that surprisingly had gone unseen. Chip's experience with his driver, and another experience earlier in his career that involved vision problems, emphasizes the importance of understanding attribution. In the sections to follow, we'll demonstrate that attribution issues can be understood and neutralized so that they do not work to your disadvantage on the golf course.

Finally, in the mental skill–building exercises that follow, keep in mind that you're learning these mental control techniques to help you during the most difficult times on the golf course—the times when it's easy for you to lose control and have it affect performance. For instance, you're playing in match play against a person who really enjoys beating you, and you must admit that you really enjoy beating that player also. He or she is a very poor winner and has just coughed during your back stroke . . . again. Other situations where controlling anxiety and anger as well as obsessiveness and perfectionism and understanding attribution would be important include the following scenarios: you find yourself obsessing over the putt you missed instead of the four putts you made; you find yourself beating yourself up after making another double bogey; you find yourself hoping not to miss the putt as you line it up; and, finally, you find yourself attributing your poor play to the need for newer and better clubs. All of the above negative thinking patterns, and the many others that you could add if you pay attention to your thoughts during a poor round of golf, contribute to that poor play. The prescriptions that follow and the exercises designed to build the suggested skills will make these and other losses of mental control less frequent, and you should quickly see improvements in your ability to "stay in the game," with improvements in your scoring as the result.

ANXIETY CONTROL PRESCRIPTION

- Stop negative thoughts and replace them with positive thoughts
- Develop imagery skills
- Understand self-hypnosis

In many ways mental control is the most paradoxical of all the problems that we have as human beings. On one hand, it seems as if it should be the simplest thing of all to be able to control the thoughts that come to our minds. As most of us know, however, it's extremely difficult to control these thoughts. As we shall discuss in this chapter and the next chapter on concentration, unless we control thoughts, performance seriously suffers, either because of the production of negative thoughts and subsequently the feelings triggered or because of the disruption in concentration (which we'll get to next chapter). Now let's look at the techniques that help us keep our thoughts positive and avoid the negative emotional and performance consequences.

Stopping Negative Thoughts

It's important to stop negative thoughts from coming into your mind. If someone else is talking to you, and in the midst of their speaking, you were to shout *Stop!*, most people would probably pause and ask you what you wanted. Some other people would keep right on speaking, unless you repeated "stop" or said it even more loudly. (Some people might not stop no matter what you did, but these are people that you probably don't want to play golf with anyway!) In most instances, though, people will stop and you would have accomplished your goal.

The person who speaks in your head, your consciousness, is very similar to another person speaking in that if you interrupt loudly enough, you probably will get the speaker within you to at least pause. By shouting *stop!* or by letting an image of a stop sign or a red stoplight come into your mind, with practice you can break up the chain of words, thoughts, or pictures that have been playing in your mind.

At this moment, while you have temporarily broken the stream of consciousness, you have the opportunity to dismiss the negative thoughts. Dismissing thoughts involves literally telling them to leave, envisioning throwing them away into the trash, or walking away from them without looking back. To keep from looking back, or more correctly, to keep from *going* back, it's important to have ready and waiting positive thoughts or images to put into the "mouth" of the speaker inside your head, or to put into your mind's eye for seeing.

The goal is to help turn around a mental control problem after it has been identified. However, preventive medicine is always better, and the practice of repeating positive self-statements, "playing" positive imagery in your mind, and reviewing your positive play on a regular basis will reduce the need for the first three prescriptions. Finally, remember to emphasize your routines, including pre-round and pre-shot routines, because these little "mini-programs" of mental and physical behavior, when executed regularly, seem to occur without much thinking, and everyone knows that the less thinking that takes place during the execution of a golf shot, the better the performance. In the next section, we'll discuss ways to practice these mental control techniques to build maximum skill and obtain maximum benefit.

Developing Imagery Skills

The kind of practice you use to develop imagery skills is somewhat different from that required in building strong self-talk skills. Most of us aren't used to thinking in pictures, although we did so as children, and only a few people regularly use imaging in their professions (e.g., interior designers, architects, painters). The rest of us don't think in pictures all that often, and the first type of practice simply involves thinking in pictures more frequently—in this case on a regular basis. We suggest that you begin with a minimum of three, although six would be better, at least five-minute practice sessions where you stop doing what you're doing, sit down, and try to visualize a scene, preferably a positive one. It's fairly easy to visualize negative scenes, and during our practice we have no desire to reinforce negative scene making. In the beginning choose only one or two scenes and practice visualizing them regularly, emphasizing as much detail as you can produce, having one imagery session build on another, and increasing the detail and the "live" qualities of the image. Virtual reality technology has given us examples of what really lifelike and detailed imagery can be, and we suggest that with regular practice your own mental "virtual reality" imagery can be nearly as vivid and compelling.

Begin pretty much "following the script" of your image, but after several practice sessions, practice adding new parts and new detail to the images on a regular basis. We have included imagery practice scripts (see appendix, page 163) that you can read and use, memorize and use, or record and use by playing the tape and following the spoken description of the developing image.

Use this type of "full-blown" imagery practice session in the beginning at least twice a day, starting with eyes closed and under optimal conditions. Later on, the frequency of the full-blown sessions can be reduced and replaced with shorter, less frequent mini-sessions and, with regular practice, you'll find that you do not need ideal conditions such as eyes closed, quiet, and no distractions to produce vivid and compelling images.

Self-Talk

The key to developing strong, controlled self-talk skills involves rehearsal of the self-talk desired, much like learning the script for a part in a play. Regular practice of that script builds control. Similarly, regular practice of self-talk dismissal procedures ("I'm not going to think about that"; "I am throwing that thought away with the garbage") is beneficial, and by paying attention to it, you'll probably be surprised how many things happen during the day that deserve dismissing.

Likewise, you want to regularly practice positive thoughts that you have decided on, possibly even written down, and which you practice regularly enough to come to mind easily. Such thoughts can include positive statements about your game on the golf course, about yourself personally, about good things that have happened in your life, and even about events in the lives of those you care about.

Self-Hypnosis

The first important thing to know about hypnosis is that *all* hypnosis is self-hypnosis. There really is no such thing as someone else, a hypnotist or hypnotherapist, hypnotizing *you*. Well-trained practitioners can instruct you and, to some degree, lead you to enter a hypnotic state, but they don't actually put you there or force you there. They simply direct and lead you, and sometimes you'll choose to go there, and sometimes you won't.

The hypnotist or hypnotherapist cannot make you do anything that you don't want to do, or ordinarily wouldn't do, but can lead you to create for yourself a state of relaxation and a state of concentration and focus which can have tremendous mental and physical control potential. This control is in all of the areas that we've been discussing in this chapter; it helps the skill of concentration and many other mental and physical processes or behaviors. Whole books have been written on the subject of hypnosis, but for our purposes we can summarize the broad benefits by saying that self-hypnosis skills can help you think better, feel better, behave more appropriately, and perform better.

To begin self-hypnosis you must first be in a suggestive or receptive state of mind and body. This is best accomplished by learning relaxation and focus techniques, such as progressive muscle relaxation, imagery-driven relaxation, autogenic phrase repetition, diaphragmatic breathing, biofeedback techniques, or yoga. The goal in this phase of preparation for self-hypnosis is to lower your arousal level and focus your attention (your mind's eye) on incoming suggestions. Suggestions can be verbal and as simple as, "I will not smoke or drink," or they can be as complicated as a whole pre-shot routine. Suggestions can be in the form of images or pictures, such as visual replay of your shot, or your play of an entire hole. Suggestions can also be a combination of thoughts and images and include emotional or sensory activity as well. For instance, you might imagine while in the relaxed and focused state that you're seeing the contour of the green more and more vividly and easily, or you might imagine that you're playing for the club championship and leading with three holes to play. In this latter instance, suggestions might involve feeling the pressure and discharging it effectively, missing a shot and recovering without losing confidence or control, or getting up and down easily from a very difficult position to win.

As with all the other techniques we have been discussing, the real power of using self-hypnosis comes from practicing it. In the beginning, practice sessions should be formal and organized. They need to be long enough to produce the low arousal and focused state and allow for several repetitions of the images or verbal suggestions. After significant skill has been built up, practice sessions can be more informed and shorter, with a few of the full "booster" sessions sprinkled in to help maintain the skill and the response.

Don't worry whether you're "under" or are actually "hypnotized." It really doesn't matter whether you achieve a trance-like state, as such a state is not necessary for skill building and for the improved performance you hope to get from your suggestions. Second, don't worry about whether in the beginning you seem like you're just observing the state and not participating in it—as if you're almost an observer of yourself, watching to determine how you're doing with the self-hypnotic exercise. This observation-like experience generally fades away with repetition.

Also, don't worry that you could hypnotize yourself and be unable to end the state or get yourself out of it. It would be impossible for you to create such a state, as the observing ego is always there even if only far in the background, to break the state of concentration, if necessary. Again, keep in mind there is nothing magical about using self-hypnosis. It's nothing to fear, nor should you look at it as a magical cure-all for your health, your game, your life, or anything else. Self-hypnosis really is just a very efficient and effective method for learning something. It combines self-help and self-control techniques and capitalizes on what we know about the nervous system and how it works and learns.

You have been in a hypnotic state many times in your life without even knowing it. As a child you probably spent many hours in a trance-like state while absorbed in your favorite TV show. When you become thoroughly engrossed in a book, you could very well drop into a trance-like state where your ability to learn, store, and access information is greater than normal. You do not have to look like you're "spaced out" or "zonked out" to be in a trance state. You will look pretty much normal to observers, though perhaps a little more peaceful and relaxed.

KEY PRINCIPLE: ACHIEVING OPTIMAL AROUSAL

There is an optimal level of physical tension or physiological arousal for the performance of any task, and this level differs for different tasks, different people, and at different times. You must learn to control your physical tension and psychological arousal if you are to improve at golf.

For many years, one of the greatest debates about performance among athletes, coaches, sport psychologists and other sport and performance scientists was about the issue of tension, fear, and anxiety and their effect on performance. Was tension or anxiety good for performance? Most everyone agreed that a player could be too tense, too anxious, and too worried about performance to perform well. There was little debate about the highest end of the tension scale. Almost any player could become paralyzed by fear and tension, and performance decline would be the expected result. The question got tougher though when the issue was moderate tension or moderate anxiety.

Fight or Flight Response

Although *tension* and *anxiety* are often used interchangeably, we're going to make a distinction here for ease of explanation. We're going to use the word *tension* for *physical tension:* the body's physiological processes speeding up as the nervous system triggers the release of adrenaline; here we see heart rate increasing, blood pressure rising, and striate muscles tightening—the familiar "fight or flight" response. The terms *fear* and *worry* usually refer more directly to mental and emotional activity, but for now, keep in mind that we will be talking primarily about the body's physiological arousal state—how physically tense or relaxed the body is—and in this case, there is a general consensus that a very high physiological arousal state almost always decreases performance.

Notice that in this last sentence we said *almost*, as it appears that there are rare exceptions to this rule. Some athletes do not seem to get too physiologically charged up to perform well. If asked which athlete is an obvious exception, many people would answer Michael Jordan. Few people would say that Jordan doesn't get better when the situation gets more difficult, when the pressure is greater, and when the game is on the line. It's clear both from his statements and his actions that he is very comfortable taking a game into his own hands. In many cases he has succeeded, sometimes in dramatic and memorable fashion.

Before we go on to the more "normal" situation where high tension levels do affect performance—let's just spend a moment asking ourselves why someone like Michael Jordan doesn't experience the kind of tensing up and "choking" that affects everyone else. Behavioral scientists know that high levels of tension decrease performance more when the tasks that one is trying to carry out are difficult. When the tasks are easier or very easy, high levels of physical tension do not decrease performance, and oftentimes will actually increase it. Michael Jordan is probably an exception to the general rule because, for him, playing basketball well— very well—is easy. It's easy because of his tremendous natural talent. It's also easy for him now because of the many years of incredibly dedicated practice and effort he has put into the game. Finally, basketball is easy for Michael because he is such an avid proponent of all three of the parts of preparation we're discussing in this book: being in great physical shape to play the game, practicing and preparing the physical skills or mechanics necessary to play well, and developing a tough mental game. It's true that with hard work and effort at developing this triad of preparation, almost any athlete can make at least some parts of any sport "easy" for them, and at least these elements of their game could actually improve while the player was experiencing high levels of tension.

Now back to the rest of us. Behavioral and sport scientists have demonstrated beyond any doubt that some physical tension is necessary for good performance. The goal of any athlete aspiring to perform his or her best is not to try to develop skills to eliminate all physician tension from play, but to feel some tension—some physiological arousal—and then use this energy, because it is energy, to their advantage in their performance. We all have experienced days when we have felt sluggish, slow, hardly awake, and clearly not focused or energized to study, to play our sport, or even to get out of bed. When we have actually gone ahead and played feeling like this, performance probably wasn't anything to "write home about." Professional baseball players don't get up for every game in a 162-game schedule, particularly those on bad teams that are going nowhere.

Professional golfers also recognize that they probably are not going to be able to get up for all tournaments, and that is one of the reasons most players on the tour play only between 50 and 75 percent of the tour events they are eligible for. Many players try to secure their spot in the top 125 on the money list to keep their playing card for the next season as early in the year as they can, so that they can pass up more tournaments later in the year in the heat of the summer and when they're beginning to wear down from the pace and the pressure. Other endurance sports like marathon running are ones that clearly demonstrate the need for one to pace oneself, both in terms of an individual race, as well as in terms of the running season.

Thus, for most of us, it's safe to say that we don't want to get too high to perform nor too low to perform and that a physical tension or physiological arousal level somewhere in between is best for most of us. Now we're not saying that everyone is the same in this regard, as there is a wide range of arousal levels in this mid-range and finding your optimal level of physical tension or arousal is one of the most important goals for the aspiring athlete, whether your sport is golf, tennis, or basketball.

Just as important as finding your level of optimal arousal for play is the realization that different sports probably require different levels, and that within a given sport there's probably a different level of physical tension or arousal that is best to perform different activities in the game. It's likely that a different level of physical tension is best for playing defense in basketball compared to the level that is best for shooting free throws. Likewise, in golf, we know that the short game, particularly putting, is greatly affected by high physical tension states, and that getting as completely relaxed as possible is probably not quite as necessary driving the ball as it is when putting.

There's an optimal level of physical tension or physiological arousal for the performance of any task, and that level differs for different tasks, for different people, and at different times. Some of your biggest goals as a golfer trying to get better should be to learn what optimal arousal is for you, then to learn to identify your arousal or tension state, and finally to learn to alter it toward the optimal for the particular task or activity in the sport you're attempting to play. As an athlete, and particularly as a golfer, you must learn how to control your physical tension, your physiological arousal level, if you are to improve at golf. Just as important to remember is that control is the ability to both raise the physical tension level when necessary or desired, and to lower the level when desired because, as we said, there are times when a somewhat higher level is better and others when a somewhat lower level of physical tension or arousal is better for performance.

Why is this the case? The answer has to do with how the body works regarding arousal levels. Part of what happens in the "fight or flight" response is that the body changes in ways that allow a person to run faster, lift more, or punch harder. Part of how the body does this is by "rerouting" blood flow into the big thick muscles of the body, somewhat shortchanging the small, more delicate muscles that are critical for execution of more delicate activities like playing the piano or putting. Part of what putters call "feel" has to do with the increased kinesthetic feedback that a person gets from an organ that receives increased blood flow through vasodilatation and relaxed muscles. This is part of the reason why it's important for athletes to be properly warmed up prior to performing because to warm up means to vasodilate and loosen up muscles. Thus, even though warming up enough before golf might not seem as critical as it might for a runner or basketball player, it's just as important, both to avoid injury and for increasing your "feel."

Finally, we could give many examples where we feel that being aware of your optimal arousal level and having the ability to control the physical tension level would be particularly important, but a few should suffice as you could undoubtedly add many yourself. It would be very important to have control of your physical tension level after your lead has been cut to one stroke with three holes to play. In this instance, the goal would be to keep the tension level from getting too high. Likewise, you would need to monitor and possibly lower the tension level if you found yourself in a position where you needed an up and down to win or to make the cut.

However, on the other end of the spectrum, if you find yourself playing in a tournament that you really didn't care much about, or playing out a round when you're already out of the competition either to win or to make the cut, you might find yourself needing to "pump yourself up" to perform at a level that you felt good about later. Finally, control of arousal level would also be particularly important when you're playing under difficult physical conditions such as in cold and windy weather. These conditions take so much out of a player that control of arousal level is not much different than the "pacing" that a marathon runner must do to complete a 26+ mile race. Controlling arousal level is a form of pacing oneself and in a 4+ hour round of golf, you must pace yourself both physically and mentally if you're not to become exhausted, burn out, and lose control of yourself on the front nine, leaving the back nine to be a potential nightmare. In the next section we will list our prescriptions for staying in control physically and the exercises that build the skills to do so.

AROUSAL CONTROL PRESCRIPTION

- Learn body-state awareness
- Lower muscle tension
- Raise arousal to optimal levels

Physical tension and arousal control is conceptually one of the simplest things that we can do to improve our golf performance. However, conceptually simple doesn't mean that it's easy to do. Gaining control over our physiological activity and arousal level can take many weeks of serious practice of the techniques that we know work if they are practiced frequently enough.

Behavioral scientists have demonstrated through the use of biofeedback training and other self-regulation techniques that humans are quite capable of gaining control over and regulating almost every body system, at least to some degree. People with high blood pressure have learned to lower their pressure without medication to safe levels. Persons with muscle tension headaches and other pain problems have greatly reduced muscle spasms and pain symptoms through muscle relaxation techniques. And persons with ulcers, colitis, or irritable bowel syndrome have greatly reduced gastrointestinal symptoms through the use of self-regulation techniques.

Compared to these uses of self-control techniques, raising or lowering your tension or arousal level is a simple business, as long as the control techniques are learned and, more important, practiced frequently enough for them to take hold and have benefit. We've included a worksheet at the end of the chapter for you to record your progress in using these techniques.

Body-State Awareness

However, before we can produce these beneficial physical changes, we must learn to do something else first that also takes practice and discipline. To be effective in gaining control over your body's arousal level, you need to learn what we call *body-state awareness*. It's difficult to change something if you don't happen to know where you are or where you started from. One of the principal benefits of the development of biofeedback techniques was their use as an assessment tool to help people become aware of what physiological state their bodies happened to be in at any given moment. What biofeedback techniques did was sharpen basic meditation techniques, which became easier because of having a tool that allowed for accurate measurement of where you started, the progress you made, and where you finished in your change process.

Turning Adversity Into Advantage

Bill Glasson

I've had four knee operations, four sinus surgeries, multiple injections in my back, periformus problems, left elbow problems, right elbow problems, . . . the list goes on and on. Many of my injuries develop from compensating for previous injuries. Others are just plain bad luck. It seems it's always just a matter of time before something else breaks down. Despite it all, I've done pretty well and had my share of success on the tour.

One of my most recent injuries (detached right forearm muscle) was the toughest one for me mentally. With the other injuries I pretty much knew what my limitations were. When I had knee problems, I changed my swing and swung most with my upper body. When I had my back ailments, I adjusted my swing (and my expectations) and was still able to hang in there. But this detached forearm thing was career threatening. I had always worked around the other problems, but with this one I just didn't know what would happen after the surgery. You know, I really thought about what else I would do, what my options were outside of playing golf. I had a bad feeling about the whole thing.

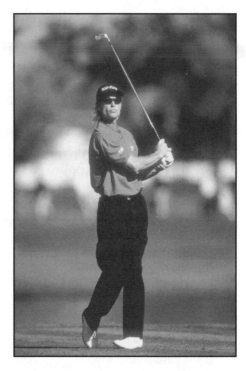

Despite my worries, things worked out in time, as they always seem to do for me. It's true that I've become smarter now than when I was younger. Back then I'd just jump right into almost anything. Nowadays I ask myself if I'm really ready. I take my time and ease into things, which I guess is just part of being older and wiser. To stick it out on the tour is hard enough in itself; to stick it out with all the injuries I've had just makes it all the more satisfying.

I now look at coming back from injuries as just one more challenge to overcome on the tour. Sure, sometimes I say, "Why me?" But most of the time I just wait it out and grin and bear it. I like having the chance to show people I can overcome any obstacle. I like to hear people say, "Bill's playing hurt again . . . and hey, he's not doing bad at all."

Over the years, my performance has been up and down. During the bad times, when you're on a losing streak and your sponsors are jumping ship, well, there are two things you can do. You can feel sorry for yourself, or you use the bad times as an incentive to show them all what you can do. I tell you, when I get in my "I'll show them" mentality, I'm a lot harder to beat.

The main thing is not getting down on yourself, not cursing your bad luck and despising others for all the good fortune and injury-free seasons they enjoy. I take it one tournament at a time, and I'm doing all right, just waiting for that next obstacle to overcome.

You need to learn to accurately access what is your physiological arousal or tension level and there are several ways you can do this without biofeedback equipment to help your control program proceed more efficiently and effectively. First, set up for yourself several ways to experience a more relaxed state than what you're likely to be used to on a normal day-to-day basis. One example would be to spend 20 minutes several times in a hot tub or whirlpool and to pay attention both to how your body feels while in the tub and how it feels directly after you get out. What you're likely to notice is that your body feels both heavy and limp, and it's also likely to feel warmer than usual. Feelings of heaviness, limpness, and warmth are frequently associated with a more relaxed body state, and these typically are feelings or sensations that you're trying to produce when you're trying to relax your body and lower your overall physical tension.

Another way to experience what relaxation feels like is to get a professional massage. These skilled therapists will successfully reduce muscle tension, reduce localized spasms, and help your body lower your overall physiological arousal level. While enjoying the massage, pay particular attention to the sensations your body produces as it relaxes.

A third way to lower tension is to wear more clothes than you normally wear and allow the increased heat retention to dilate blood vessels and produce a lower arousal state. Again, you're using these techniques primarily to get acquainted with how your body feels when it's more relaxed and in a lower tension state, although you should note that by doing so you actually help train your body to be able to enter these states more easily and quickly. Thus, these exercises help you to develop solid physical control skills both by helping you become more aware of the state you're trying to produce, and by actually helping your body enter these states more frequently and more easily, "paving the way" so to speak for a good response to your practice exercises. A worksheet at the end of the chapter will help you record your progress as you practice the exercises.

Lowering Muscle Tension

To produce the actual physical changes, some systems seem to be easier to change than others. It's important to learn to produce lowered muscle tension, one of the easier systems to train with practice. Progressive muscle relaxation exercises involve tensing up a muscle group, holding its tension level while it fatigues, paying attention to how it feels at that level of activity, and then releasing the muscle tension all at once, allowing it to drop down below its starting point and for a few moments become more relaxed than it had been prior to the procedure. This exercise gives you the opportunity to experience the different muscle tension states, and with frequent repetition the muscle gradually becomes trained to release muscle tension better. Over time the resting level of muscle tension gradually becomes lower and lower. The exercise is a simple one of going through the body one muscle group at a time, carrying out this flexing, holding, observing, releasing, and observing exercise with enough repetitions to produce the lower tension- level effect.

Another physical tension-lowering technique is the use of a breathing technique often taught in Lamaze classes, to athletes by coaches or other instructors, or to singers by voice coaches because of the varied benefits that the breathing technique produces for those using it. The technique is called diaphragmatic breathing and it involves using the abdominal muscles to extend the abdomen upon inhalation allowing oxygen to passively enter the lungs. The breathing cycle is completed by contracting the abdominal muscles upon exhalation, thus more actively pushing the deoxygenated air out of the lungs. This respiratory pattern is one which is hooked up to the mechanisms in the body which combine to lower overall physiological arousal, in contrast with chest or backward breathing where one inhales by expanding the chest which contributes to a physiological tensing of the body, the pumping of adrenaline, and activation of our fight or flight response. There are numerous other benefits of diaphragmatic breathing besides being one of the most effective techniques for lowering tension levels, including improved digestion and autoimmune system function. But for our purposes, learning to be an effective diaphragmatic breather is one of the most beneficial techniques if you're trying to improve your golf performance. With regular practice, this technique becomes a useful one to do because it requires no tools, no equipment, and no special locations to carry out, and it's always available to the golfer on the golf course to help lower physical tension levels quickly and easily, thus allowing the golfer to regulate his or her physiological arousal level closer to that optimum point for performance. As you have seen, deep diaphragmatic breaths play a significant role in our pre-shot routine.

Raising Arousal to Optimal Levels

We have now talked about two simple methods for lowering arousal levels. As we stated previously, it's also important to be able to raise arousal level when desired. You would want to raise arousal level when you notice that you're feeling and playing "flat," when you notice that you seem distracted and "not with it," or when you're desiring a burst of energy to get that extra 10 yards out of your tee ball. It is probably in football where you see the most obvious evidence of physical activity that is designed to "pump up" the athlete for performance. Before games, and sometimes on the sidelines during games, we often see players chest-bumping each other, slapping each other, or even butting their heads. As a golfer, you probably are not going to engage in this Neanderthal-looking behavior, nor do you need to produce "pumping up" in this manner. Remember above, where we talked about the opposite of diaphragmatic breathing, we called it chest or backward breathing. This "pump up" breathing pattern involves expanding your chest when you inhale as you would necessarily do if you were holding your stomach in (remember "chest out, stomach in" as in the military or at the beach). This breathing pattern triggers automatic activity, and will raise heart rate and blood pressure, tense muscles, and prepare you to run, fight, or "grip it and rip it."

When you have practiced these two different breathing patterns with two different effects on your body's arousal level, you have with you a simple tool to raise or lower your body tension and arousal level on command. We suggest that you try some chest/pump up breathing on the tee if you have found that your optimal arousal level for driving is fairly high. However, whether your optimal level is on the higher end or the lower end of the range for optimal performance, it's likely that good, deep diaphragmatic breaths will most likely help chipping, wedge play, and putting.

Finally, whichever of the tension-level regulation techniques you settle on, be sure to include them in both your pre-round and pre-shot routines to use them to your advantage. In the next section, we'll get more specific about setting up exercises to develop these very important body-control skills.

Controlling Your Tension and Relaxation States

The exercises involved in physical tension control can be done with or without tools to assist the process. First, diaphragmatic breathing should be practiced many times a day, with a few five- to ten-minute practice sessions and numerous one- to two-minute ones until the in-and-out movement of the abdominal muscles feels normal or natural, and the breathing pattern becomes the primary one used. A simple technique that can be used to make the learning of diaphragmatic breathing easier is to lie down or sit down and place one hand on your stomach and the other on your chest. Next, try to inhale by pushing your abdomen out, which should push against the lower hand and push it out as well, without moving the chest or the upper hand. Exhalation should involve the stomach and the lower hand moving in, again without any movement by the chest or by the upper hand.

Sometimes the diaphragmatic breathing pattern feels awkward to people when first practicing it. Though it may feel awkward, it's by no means unnatural. It is in fact the way infants and small children breathe (unlike many adults who suck in their stomachs to appear slimmer). When the stomach is held in, your breathing has to go somewhere and the movement goes up into the chest and becomes the chest or backward breathing discussed earlier. The "chest out, stomach in" of the military, and otherwise thrusting your chest out to look more muscular, bustier, and/or thinner, contributes to chest or backward breathing being the most common pattern for most American adults. Unfortunately this breathing pattern that is designed for fight or flight purposes becomes the most common and "natural pattern" for adults. The downside of this pattern is that it keeps people more physiologically tense than they need to be, and the resulting elevated tension level neither feels particularly good nor is it as healthy as the lower arousal state of diaphragmatic breathing.

If you practice this simple diaphragmatic breathing exercise frequently it will begin to feel like your normal way to breathe. At the point where it begins to feel automatic, you might actually have to consciously and purposefully activate chest or backward breathing when you want a higher arousal state. Thus, with practice, you should be able to achieve what is almost the reverse of the situation in which most people start diaphragmatic breathing practice, that is, consciously and purposefully having to work at diaphragmatic breathing while chest breathing unconsciously, and with the practice of the diaphragmatic breathing bringing about the reverse.

Again killing two birds with one stone, your exercise for increasing physical tension or physiological arousal, your "pump-up" breathing exercise is in fact the reverse of what you do for diaphragmatic breathing. You can again place one hand on your chest and one on your stomach and this time expand the chest, force the upper hand out when you inhale without moving your stomach, and retract the chest and upper hand upon exhalation. If you do that several times rapidly you will notice that you might even feel somewhat dizzy from it. If you were to do it rapidly for a few moments, you would get a little taste of how it feels to hyperventilate. (We don't suggest that you do this, however.)

Remember that because you're probably using chest or backward breathing most of the time now, you're likely to need much more practice with the diaphragmatic exercise than with the backward breathing one to effectively equip yourself with both techniques for tension control. Once you have both breathing patterns down pat and can do either when you wish upon command, try using them purposefully before different shots out on the golf course and see if you find that one of the patterns or the other seems to help your shot making. Most likely, you will find that the chest or backward breathing pattern is more helpful when you're trying to drive the ball whether off the tee or from the fairway, and the diaphragmatic pattern more helpful for your short game.

A progressive muscle-relaxation exercise involves flexing one muscle group at a time, paying attention to the feelings that it produces, holding that tension for a six to eight count, and then releasing the muscle to allow it to unwind so that you can feel the difference. In the beginning it's best to do this exercise one muscle group at a time, such as bending your wrist down, keeping your fist clenched, and feeling the tension. You could begin with one wrist and fist or both, whichever is your preference, and then after a while expand the area that you're working on—for instance wrists, fists, and forearms. At this point you could gradually work your way up your arms to include your shoulders and neck muscles. You could then focus specifically on stomach muscles or low back muscles and again, flex, hold, study the tension, release, and study the sensations that releasing tension brings. For your convenience we have included in the appendix a full progressive muscle-relaxation script for you to use to practice this exercise.

Note that the more you practice the more you notice that you can not only better discriminate when muscles are tense and when they have relaxed, but you will also notice that some muscles relax with fewer repetitions of tensing and releasing than others and that some will be more resistant than others to this relaxation process. Because you have a script to follow, keep in mind that you can adapt that script by going over and repeating some of the muscle groups that seem to be the most resistant for you, thus tailoring your exercise to help you get beyond troublesome muscle groups. Finally, because you have a script that has been written word-by-word, it is one that you can make an audio tape recording of, and once made, you can sit back and practice it by following the instructions on the tape. Keep in mind that you also could make several tapes, altering the exercise to skip some muscle groups, and/or increase repetitions of others for greater practice effects.

Last, we want to say just a few words about other low arousal-producing techniques such as yoga, meditation, and biofeedback. All these techniques are beneficial and whether you take the time to learn them either by taking a course, by purchasing an instructional book, audio, or video series, or by seeking out a behavioral scientist who specializes in the instruction of these activities, any of them can produce for you an increased ability to create a lower physical tension state that would be beneficial for you. However, if you practice the diaphragmatic and muscle relaxation exercises we suggest in this book, you probably won't need to go out and buy instructions for these other more complicated procedures.

As in previous chapters, we have included a worksheet to help you practice these physical tension-control exercises. In addition, as mentioned earlier, we have included a progressive muscle relaxation exercise that you can use by reading it and referring to it when you practice, by memorizing it and practicing it verbatim, or by audiotaping it and following along as you play the tape back in practice.

figure 4.1 STAYING IN CONTROL (PHYSICALLY) WORKSHEET

Days/Carried out procedure

Physical control procedures	M	TU	W	TH	F	SA	SU
Diaphragmatic breathing							
Backward pump-up breathing							
Progressive muscle relaxation							
Pump up / Muscle tensing							
Imagery / Relaxation							
Suggestion / Hypnosis							

Criteria: Carried out procedure = Yes ; didn't = No

Reward criteria: Carried out at least _____ procedures _____ times per _____.

Reward: _____

Figure 4.2 STAYING IN CONTROL (MENTALLY AND EMOTIONALLY) WORKSHEET

Days/Carried out procedure

Mental/ Emotional control procedures	M	TU	W	TH	F	SA	SU
Self-talk							
Imagery							
Thought stopping							
Dismissing							
Desensitization							
Suggestions / Hypnosis							
Attribution							
Rehearsal							

Criteria: Carried out procedure = Yes ; didn't = No

Reward criteria: Carried out at least _____ procedures _____ times per _____.

Reward: _____

chapter
5

Fine-Tuning Your Focus

The Snakes and the Shakes

Mike Small

Mike Small, a promising young player on the PGA tour, was playing in a tournament on the Asian tour several years ago. At a tournament in Thailand, Mike was faced with many of the difficulties that plague American or European golfers in playing events in the Far East: time-change and jet-lag difficulties, significant dietary difficulties, language and other cultural problems, and difficult weather conditions. Mike had prepared for these expected adversities and for the first several

rounds had done well at blocking them out, keeping his focus and concentration. He was in competition in the tournament. While studying a difficult putt on a green on the back nine, an unfamiliar noise broke into Mike's concentration and disrupted his pre-shot routine for his putt. Feeling the presence of something behind him, Mike slowly turned to see a large king cobra (not the driver!) directly within striking distance. Mike slowly got himself out of the snake's range, and play resumed after the snake was removed. Unfortunately, Mike couldn't get the close call out of his mind. He missed that putt and several putts afterward, and he was soon out of contention in the tournament. That was Mike's last tournament in Asia and he has vowed not to return there to play. After hearing of this incident, we couldn't think of a better reason for working on your concentration and mental skills to stay on the PGA tour and avoid ever having to play in front of that kind of gallery.

Concentration Control

Perceptual psychologists talk about an important concept called "figure-ground" that relates to attention and concentration. Whatever we're attending to or focused on is called the "figure," and everything else is described as being in the background, or "ground." As you read this book, if you're focused on and taking in what you're reading, the book and its information is the figure and everything else around you is the ground.

If you find the book interesting, and if you're in a quiet place with few other distractions, it should be relatively easy for you to keep the book and its information as the figure and not have your attention drift elsewhere—the book and the information drifting out of your awareness into the "ground" and, as often happens in this instance, with little of the reading or information learned or retained. If you're reading this book in a place where there's a television on with loud volume and where you can see the picture out of the corner of your eye, it would be much more difficult to keep the book and the information in the figure and keep the television program in the background (especially if it's one of your favorite television shows!). You could demonstrate these principles by continuing your reading under different conditions, reading at times with more distractions than other times, and noticing the difference in how easy the reading is and how much is retained.

KEY PRINCIPLE: CONCENTRATION

To succeed in golf, you need to keep your attention on the task at hand, focus on the important aspects of events, and intensify your concentration to a point where distractions do not disrupt it.

For several reasons, concentration principles may play a more important role in golf than in any other sport. First, there's so much time between golf shots during a round that it would be almost impossible to keep concentrating on golf for every second of a four-hour round. Second, during that four-hour round, there are really only a few minutes of actual play—that is, swinging the club—with the remainder of the time spent walking from one spot on the course to another, waiting for others to play. Compare this to basketball, a game that ordinarily takes about two hours to complete, in which starters on the team are actively involved for 30 to 40 minutes of that time. Third, golf is the most active, as opposed to reactive, sport, in that in almost all other sports, except perhaps bowling, golfers initiate the action without having to react to a ball hit, kicked, or thrown at them. In other sports, like wrestling, much of the action is in response to a physical action or reaction by an opponent. Not so in golf. In many ways, this difference makes golf less like a typical sport and more like taking an exam before which you study, prepare, get yourself as physically and mentally prepared for the execution of your skills as possible, and then demonstrate what you know and execute what you can do.

Coming up with examples of the role of attention, concentration, and focus during golf was one of the easiest tasks in writing this book. Each of us probably experiences a dozen instances during each round of golf where good concentration helps us and poor control of our attention and our focus hurts us. A professional at the Masters, a high school or college player at a conference tournament, or a club player at a club championship may very well play in front of a sizable gallery. It is well recognized that galleries make noise, and that noise can be distracting enough to ruin your concentration when you're attempting to perform. The situation is doubly difficult if the gallery is both large and noisy, and you're in contention to win (galleries tend to get larger and noisier around players in contention). Thus, if you're in a position to win, you will likely have a greater chance of success if you can focus on the shot at hand, keep your mind on your pre-shot routine, and block out the gallery.

Fighting the Past

It's extremely difficult to concentrate on the shot at hand when you're shooting over water on a hole where you put two in the water the last time you played! In this type of situation, your memories work against you. Thoughts of the past creep into the present and contaminate your concentration with anxiety and disappointment from your previous experience. These contaminating thoughts also carry with them anger and frustration from the past, and the triggering of these strong emotions while you're attempting to concentrate and execute a shot is further complicating. Imagine the feelings of the tour player participating in the Tournament Players Championship at Sawgrass in Florida when he walks from the 16th green to the 17th tee, the infamous hole where you hit completely over water to the island green. During that short walk that must seem like miles, the player must concentrate on executing the shot at hand and keep thoughts of previous balls hit long or short or left or right into the water (their own shots or those hit by other players) out of his thoughts. If he can't clear his thoughts of these memories, the chances of their repeating are greatly increased.

Fighting the Future

Similar to thinking about past problems on the golf course is thinking ahead to future potential problems. For instance, fear of the water on 17 at the TPC often begins long before you approach that feared tee box. Even before the tournament begins, Chip has commented on his difficulty in not thinking about two particularly troublesome holes for him at the Coal Valley Country Club in the Quad Cities Tournament in Moline, Illinois. Chip has had particular difficulty with these two holes, and he has had to work hard at strengthening his concentration prior to this tournament because of the tendency for these two holes to break into his focus and create problems. It's interesting that the two holes at Coal Valley are not two of the toughest holes on the course, but for a given player, personal difficulties with a hole can produce a mental block and make it very difficult to concentrate on execution.

Zoning Out

An elite college golfer recently mentioned a form of concentration loss not caused by a noisy gallery, memories of poor outings, or worry about what's ahead. In his instance, it wasn't a case of negative thoughts breaking into his consciousness and disrupting focus, but a situation in which his mind went blank, and he simply lost touch with what he was concentrating on and attempting to carry out. It's like being a student in class who suddenly notices that she's not reading or thinking about anything, that she's just staring at the lecturer without absorbing anything that has been said. The college player said that when he "blanked out" he invariably made more mistakes in club selection and in identifying the important factors on the course, such as changing wind conditions. He would misread greens and feel overall as if he were no longer actually competing in the tournament. Sometimes, he said, this mental blankness becomes even more pronounced and is like a condition that psychologists call "dissociation," where his thoughts and feelings make him feel as if he is not actually participating in the event but rather watching it from the outside.

It's safe to say that the ability to keep your mind on what you want it to be on, and off everything else for an extended period of time, is a skill particularly important in golf, since this skill is so highly correlated with successful shot making. In the next section we'll discuss how to gain mastery over your attention and focus and how to get concentration to work to your advantage in practice and competition.

Practicing Mind Control

Before you control your attention, concentration, and focus, you need to understand what you're attempting to control. Try this: stop reading at the end of this sentence and let yourself become aware of, and then try to describe to yourself, what you're thinking about.

How long were you gone? Can you describe what you were thinking during that time? If you're like most people, you may have found that what's typically on your mind is a loosely organized, often fragmented stream of words, accompanied by images. What you were focusing on, the *figure* we described earlier, was the ongoing activity of your conscious mind, often called your "stream of consciousness." It is usually only roughly a stream; more often it's made up of little fragments of ideas, information, or commentary, usually about what you're seeing or doing or are otherwise involved in.

When we're very engrossed in something, the information or "data" stream in our consciousness is much less fragmented; it is much more like a stream traveling from one point to another. When this data stream is coherent, linear, and directed, it is often much more productive for us. Interspersed in this verbal data stream are occasional pictures instead of words, and when we purposefully decide to think in pictures, or imagine, we can be very good at producing vivid and complex three-dimensional images of objects or events. Actually, the new virtual reality technology gives us an even better way to describe this imaging capability, as the pictures are much more like three-dimensional movies in which we are participating.

This stream-of-consciousness verbal and imagined mental activity is both one of our biggest assets and biggest liabilities as human beings. Control of the stream of mental activity gives us tremendous potential to play golf and do most other things well; on the other hand, a lack of control of the stream, when it fragments, makes it difficult to focus long enough on the activity to do it well. We discussed earlier some of the consequences of loss of control over the stream of consciousness including its contamination by thoughts of negative past events or future potential ones, or simply the intrusion and breakup of the consciousness stream by unwanted competing stimuli such as noise, crowds, or illness.

On the positive side, control of the data stream of consciousness is what we call *concentration,* and good control of it results in several benefits, including rapid learning, effective information storage and retrieval, rapid and effective use of important higher mental processes such as analysis and decision making, and the ability to anticipate future events and their outcomes. In a sense you can experience the future in the present and change your reactions to future events because of your ability to rehearse responses to them. This last ability—to imagine events and experience them as if they were really happening—has tremendously important and far-reaching implications for your ability to self-regulate your thoughts, feelings, and actions and to reduce deficits and improve performance. Thus, as we talk about the prescription for fine-tuning your focus, keep in mind that conscious self-control of attention, concentration, focus, and this stream of consciousness has potential not only for improving your golf game but also for helping you perform well in many other areas.

CONCENTRATION PRESCRIPTION

- Stay in the present
- Rehearse routines to eliminate distractions

Stay in the Present

The shot that you have at hand is the only shot that can affect your score, your round, or how you finish in a tournament. Neither the shot you have just completed nor the next shot deserves your focus. Only the *present* shot needs your focus. From when you first approach your ball until the swing has been completed, the ball has landed and stopped rolling, and you have reviewed the shot (and either stored it because you liked it or dismissed it because you didn't), you are in the present. We could call this period from approach through review "on" time (as opposed to "off" time, which is the rest of your time on the course, including walking between shots). When you're "on," you want to be focusing on the current shot and no other. During off time between shots it's fine to focus on a previous shot that you hit well, other thoughts or images that are positive, or even nongolf-related issues or activities, particularly ones that conserve your energy and help keep you upbeat. But during your "on" time of the current shot, *all* thoughts other than those involving the shot are in a sense negative thoughts, because they break in and disrupt your pre-shot routine or shot mechanics.

Again, it's essential to stay in the present only during your "on" time versus your "off" time, when you may wish to let down your focus in order to conserve energy. But once you begin your approach, you're "on" again, and from this point you focus only on the shot at hand. Practicing this kind of concentration will protect you from the disease of indecision, the contamination of negative or worrisome thoughts, the cold chill of anticipatory anxiety for potential trouble ahead, and the huge cost of a loss of focus.

Rehearse Routines to Eliminate Distractions

The key to eliminating distractions is to make sure that you have regularly rehearsed and practiced to the point of automatic pre-shot mental and physical routines. It's much easier to control thoughts when you're thinking a well-rehearsed and constructed set of sequential thoughts and images. Think about it. We all know how difficult it is to attempt to break up a string of thoughts in our stream of consciousness. One example is when you hear a song on the radio and then have difficulty getting the song out of your head.

Many people are bothered by repetitive, obsessive thoughts. A goal of a solid pre-shot routine is to keep your mind moving forward in a straight line through your mental and physical preparation for the shot and to make it difficult for that mental activity "stream" to be disrupted by distracting thoughts and feelings. Recall our discussion of the steps of your pre-shot routine—you saw that one step builds on the next as you progress in your preparation to make the desired shot.

Rehearsing your routine also involves on-the-course distraction elimination and dealing with instances where your pre-shot routine has failed and there has been an intrusion of negative or disruptive thoughts into the data stream of your consciousness. When this occurs you need a prepared mental emergency "videotape" that includes positive statements about your talents, abilities, and desire, as well as images of your past successes (golf and nongolf) that have been regularly practiced so that they can come to mind when you need them. Keeping in reserve these mental "emergency" measures will give you the advantage of being able to counteract the negative intrusions and get your mind and focus back on track before much damage is done.

The Intangibles

Fred Funk

When you're not playing well, your "lens" becomes wider and you see a lot more stuff than you want to. You're more conscious of what you're doing with yourself, with your body and all your movements, and you're not letting it flow. I think what they call the "zone" is just anxiety-free golf.

Unfortunately, you can't make flow happen. After it's gone, you wonder how you got it and what you did to lose it. You say, "Wow, I just had this great stretch—what happened? What was I doing right? Why was I playing so well? How do I get there again?" But if you try to regain the flow, you lose focus and start to screw everything up.

I think the toughest thing out here, though, is not wondering whether you're going to make $800,000 or $1 million but whether you're going to keep that card. You're always an injury or a bad year away. If you don't have any exemptions running with you, there just isn't any job security out here. That's something that's always in the back of my mind. I've got to stay that much sharper than 80% of the guys out here so that I can beat 'em. Sometimes I can't beat 'em on talent, but I can beat them on intestinal fortitude—that's what I've gotta do a lot of times. There's always that intangible. You see guys that hit the ball unbelievably well and they never make their card and other guys that scrap all over the place, they never really hit a solid shot, but they have great games, win majors, and they are constant winners out here. You say, "What's that guy have? How come he's doing all this and the other guy isn't?" But you can't measure what's inside a person. And that's the biggest thing out here—what's inside and your belief in yourself. Do you believe that when you're playing well that you're good enough to win out here? I think until you win you're wondering and then when you win the first time, you ask yourself, "Well, was that luck?" I think the second one is harder than the first one. It was for me. The first one in Houston came out of nowhere. I missed a bunch of cuts in a row, and I pulled out of Greensboro the week before Houston. I was getting resumes ready, job applications, thinking about going back into coaching. I was telling myself I wasn't ready for the tour. And then the next week, I won. It was like, "Where did that come from?" And all of a sudden, I'm saying, "Hmmm, I guess I'm good enough now!"

Controlling Your Concentration

As we said earlier, concentration is a cognitive or mental skill somewhat similar to memory. Like memory, concentration can be improved by practicing mental activities that strengthen and sharpen specific mental skills. We can best think of improving and strengthening concentration by thinking of the data stream of consciousness that we talked about earlier as a path in our minds where we try to take our thinking from one point straight to another without wavering. If we think about this desired path in our minds as similar to a path that people walk on, the more the path is taken, the more it gets "grooved" into the ground, and the more likely that most people will walk the path to get from the first point to the second. To improve concentration, your goal is to practice desired thinking regularly under various conditions until the desired thoughts come to mind easily and can be completed without the stream of consciousness leaving the grooved path and losing direction (or being contaminated by other thought patterns, as we discussed earlier).

Concentration Drills

We've developed several exercises that help "groove" your thoughts so that you can begin the goal-directed thought pattern and follow through with it all the way to the goal without disruption, contamination, or diversion into an unwanted thought pattern. The first exercise involves sharpening your attention and making it less easy to contaminate. A television and videotape recorder are useful, but you can do the exercise without them.

First, watch and record on videotape several minutes of commercials. After you have watched them once and recorded them, turn the TV and VCR off, find a paper and a pencil, and write down as much as you can remember about what you heard and saw in the most minute detail that you can. (See Figure 5.1.) After this, rewind the tape and replay the commercials to see how accurate you were the first time. Compare what you thought you saw and heard to what really did occur. Note how many correct details and how many incorrect ones you recalled. Do this short exercise with other taped commercials at least twice a day, a thirty minute total time commitment. Very quickly, you should notice that your attention to detail improves, and your number of visual and auditory "mistakes" decreases.

To do the exercise without a TV and VCR, try this: wherever you may happen to be reading this book, put it down for a moment. Find paper and a pencil, and give yourself two minutes to concentrate on everything that is in front of you at this moment. After two minutes, turn and face the other direction, and write down all that you remember seeing. After you have written down everything you can remember, turn back around to check for completeness and accuracy. Perform this exercise many times in many different settings, and you'll soon notice improvements in your attention to detail.

After several consecutive days of this exercise, you'll begin to get sharper in noticing details and staying focused on what you desire to pay attention to. After a few weeks of practice, try making the task more difficult by introducing distractions into your practice session. One way of doing this is to add to the television and VCR exercise a distraction such as a radio playing while you're trying to focus on the television commercial. To make the exercise even more difficult, blast the radio and also ask someone to talk to you while you try to focus on the TV. The more obstacles to your focus that you can ignore, the stronger and sharper your mental skills become.

Course Observation Drills

Once you've done the previous exercise several times, you can try taking your practice to the course. During a round of recreational golf with friends, for the first nine holes, play only the odd-numbered holes. On the even-numbered holes, rather than playing the hole, simply observe the course, the conditions, the way your partner plays the hole, and other details that you happen to notice. After completing the nine holes, take 10 minutes and write down as much as you can remember about each hole. (See Figure 5.2.)You may notice that you have become more "in touch" with the even-numbered holes that you didn't play than the odd-numbered holes that you did play. On the back nine, play the even-numbered holes and observe the odd, and follow the nine with the same written review exercise. You'll probably notice that you were more focused and paid more attention on the holes that you played on the back nine than you did on the front nine.

A related exercise that is easy to do is to ask your playing partner to purposefully attempt to distract you during your round. Have him or her bring up topics that are distracting for you, possibly even ones that upset you or evoke other emotional responses. This will get you some practice both in blocking out conversation and dealing with your disruptive emotions.

You might also introduce friendly wagers to disrupt your concentration. Because you're doing this purposefully to work on concentration, the wagers will not be as much pressure or as disrupting as they would be otherwise. This is because, as human beings, we have the ability to mediate our emotional response to some degree, and since this was purposeful practice, the pressure that we would feel would be moderate and recognized as positive because we're wanting it to be there to work on. Still, this is a good exercise for overcoming distraction, and it helps somewhat in desensitizing you to pressure.

Focus on the Positive

Lee Janzen

We're *always* concentrating on something. It's just whether or not it's the right thing. Everything I do, I do continuously. I do the same things over and over again—it's just that much easier to be right in that routine. So when I get out on the course, I know each shot is just as important as another. All I'm trying to do is think of what I want to do with this shot. What is the best shot? And then that's the shot I try to hit. You've got 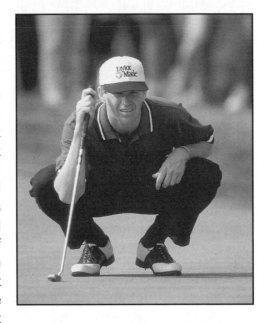 to forget about the bad shots, forget about all past shots, and go with the current shot as it is. It's the only shot you're going to play that moment, and it's the only shot you can do anything about.

I used to get all wrapped up when I'd miss shots or when I'd get a bad break here and there. It just doesn't do you any good. I've also found that once you start talking about one bad break, suddenly you're thinking backward the whole time, and all you're thinking is, "Man, I can't get a break today." So now I focus on the shot ahead of me and how I'm going to hit as good a shot as I possibly can. It doesn't matter where the ball ends up. I can only do the best I can. Whatever you focus on becomes real. So if you think about being unlucky, you're going to be unlucky. If you think about being lucky, you're also going to be unlucky. But if you think about the shot at hand, you'll make your own luck.

Focusing Drills

Another exercise to improve concentration involves narrowing and widening your focus, making more specific or broader what's in the figure of your concentration as opposed to what's in the ground (using the terms of perceptual psychology introduced earlier). Put this book down right where you're sitting and focus your mind's eye on whatever is in front of you. Pick a spot, such as a point on a picture, and focus your gaze and your attention very specifically on that point. Now widen what you're focused on to include the whole picture minus the frame. Next, widen your focus to include the whole picture with the frame. Now, if there happen to be several pictures on the wall, allow your focus to be on all of the pictures, but not on the space between them. Next, let your focus widen to include the whole wall. Next, allow your focus to be on the whole wall but not on the pictures. In this instance, you will see that your mind can screen out the pictures from the wall and allow the wall to be the figure and the pictures the ground.

Now go in the reverse direction, narrowing your focus back to the outer border of the pictures. Then reverse the focus to include only the space between the pictures and not the pictures themselves. Next, shrink the focus down to one picture and then the single spot, and then widen the focus again in the same manner. In doing this, you are exercising your brain's ability to change focus, narrowing and widening it at your command.

You can also do this exercise at the golf course. You can narrow your focus down to the landing area for your drive, your target line, the borders of the fairway minus the first cut or rough, or the whole panorama out in front of you. You can also narrow down to just the fairway minus the sand traps or the water. If you can do this, then you are using your mind to block out these hazards and play the hole as if these obstacles were not there.

Remember that your mind can do these rather sophisticated tasks only with practice. Don't expect them to work for you perfectly the first time. If you stick with them, these exercises will pay off, with interest. It's only the lack of practice of this kind of activity that makes it difficult for you to screen out hazards to avoid disruption of your concentration and shot routine.

Imagery Techniques

Finally, another useful concentration technique is replaying a hole in your mind, in images or pictures, that you have played often. With practice of this imagining exercise, you can expand the technique to playing an entire round mentally. With this type of concentration practice, you'll soon see that you can remember more detail of the whole round—and the more detail of play that you can imagine, the more your nervous system will accept the imagined play as real play. In this way, imagined play does not differ significantly from actual play.

Once you've reached a level of mental practice where you can play a whole round in imagery in your mind, you now have the opportunity to play imaginary rounds—rounds that have not actually occurred. With this skill, you can imagine rounds played exactly as you would wish them to be, even if you may have never played a round so effectively. This practice allows you to work on your game even when you're not actually playing and to rehearse imagined positive play in such a way that your nervous system comes to believe that the round actually happened. At this point the positive play is no longer outside of possibility, it is in the "eye" of the nervous system, something very possible and do-able, and in some sense the system reacts as if this positive play has already occurred. Once you achieve this level of control and can carry out this practice, you're preparing much more like the pros do, and you have a much greater chance of playing like they do on the golf course.

Figure 5.1 **FINE-TUNING YOUR FOCUS: SAMPLE WORKSHEET #1**

Key principle or skill: *Concentration strengthening*

Describe exercise:
1. Use a TV and VCR to sharpen attention to details.
2. Use a TV, VCR, and radio to sharpen concentration when distractions are present.

Materials needed: TV, VCR, radio

Procedure:

Concentration   1. Tape several 4-minute segments of commercials; play a 4-minute segment; record details; replay to check accuracy; play another segment or two and try to improve number and accuracy.

Distraction   2. As number 1 above adding radio distractions.

Goal(s): *Increase number and accuracy of details.*
Reward 25% increases (percent correct details minus percent incorrect details.

Rewards for goals attained:
1. Sleeve of balls
2. New visor
3. New putter

Practice sessions:

Sessions								
Activity	1	2	3	4	5	6	7	8
Concentration TV/VCR	30	25	29	35	21	35	48	42
Distraction TV/VCR/radio	18	29	21	29	46*	40	45	58*

(Score: % correct details — % incorrect details)

* Rewards given

Figure 5.2 FINE-TUNING YOUR FOCUS: SAMPLE WORKSHEET #2

Key principle or skill: *Concentration strengthening*

Describe exercise:
While playing 18 holes with a friend, practice playing while your friend engages in distracting activities.

Procedure:
Ask your friend to talk, move around within sight, make noises, or do other distracting activities when you are playing even holes only. Compare odd holes.

Goal(s): *Increase concentration so that distractions do not affect play on even holes compared to odd holes.*

Rewards for goals attained:
Deposit $20.00 toward new clubs for each round distraction is successfully blocked out.

Practice sessions:

	Sessions							
Activity	1	2	3	4	5	6	7	8
Even holes score	61	58	53	49	51	47*	44*	44
Odd holes score	48	47	48	45	47	48	46	42

* Rewards given

Figure 5.3 FINE-TUNING YOUR FOCUS WORKSHEET

Key principle or skill: _____

Describe exercise: _____
_____
_____

Materials needed:_____
_____
_____

Procedure: _____
_____
_____

Goal(s): _____
_____
_____

Rewards for goals
attained: _____
_____
_____

Practice sessions:

Sessions								
Activity	1	2	3	4	5	6	7	8

* Rewards given

chapter

6

Performing Under Pressure

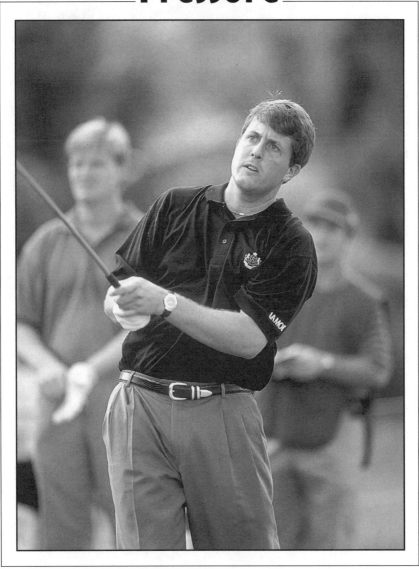

Shooting 59

Chip Beck

I shot a 59 in the fourth round of the 1991 Las Vegas Invitational. I don't want to brag (well, maybe a little), but as of this writing in the summer of 1998, no one since has shot a 59 in a PGA Tour tournament.

The night before, my caddie and I went out to the golf course and saw a few players around the putting green. They were putting and chipping, and two of them were talking about the prize for a 59. "You watch," one of them said. "Some-

body might shoot 59 this week. This course is not as tough as some. You get a lot of birdies, and you can get to the par fives in two." Earlier that week, my caddie had walked the course. When he came back, he said that the course could give us a good score. I don't think he had ever been quite so prophetic.

We went home that night and didn't think much of it other than just participating, having a good round, and getting back into the tournament. As it turned out the next day, the 59 put me in a position to win the tournament. In the end I got third, but the 59 made it a good week for me.

After sinking my putt on the 15th green, I was sitting at 50 even. I knew I had to birdie the next three holes to shoot 59. I was feeling the pressure. Earlier, when I was making the turn to the back nine, one of the marshals said, "Gosh, that was the best score on this side by about two strokes, and you've got the easier side coming." "Oh, man, that's great," I said. But it puts a little pressure on you. I started out birdying a few holes on the back side. The only time I was really in trouble was when I got a little nervous on a par three. I hit a chip from the edge of the green about 10 feet past the hole, and I had a very difficult putt coming back to make it. I knew I had to make it. Fortunately, I stuck to my routine and was able to sink that putt. That was a good par. But after that I still had to birdie the last few holes to shoot a 59.

As it came down to the last hole, I really tried to shoot it. It was nerve-wracking just trying to get the ball onto the fairway. I was nervous, *really* nervous. Luckily, I drove it very nicely; my routine really carried me. Then, on the next shot, I knew the greens were bumpy and there was no guarantee I could make a putt of any length, so I decided to try the shot from the fairway. The shot was in between clubs. I thought my ball would come up a little high over the bunker, so I figured that I'd probably have a better chance stopping it near the hole with an eight iron. It came out very well. It looked to me that the ball had hit right next to the hole and just sat there, but because the green was a little bit elevated, I couldn't tell for sure. When I got up there, I just said, "Oh, wow!" From the way people had been clapping and carrying on around the green, I had thought the putt would be a "tap in," but in fact I had a pretty tough downhill left-to-right putt with what looked like some feet marks in the way. It was going to be a tough putt to make.

Recognizing the moment, the amateurs I was playing with were scurrying around and saying, "What do you want us to do? We just want to get out of here and out of your way." The amateurs picked up, and I went to the side of the green and gathered myself. I decided that I would just give it the best chance I could. I would settle myself enough to just give it a chance. That was all I could do. I hit the putt very well. It could have gone either way, but it caught the edge of the hole and went in. It had curved right and fallen in on the right side of the hole. It was a very good putt, I felt, because it could have done anything at that point. It could have bumped a little farther right, but I hit it well enough that it had a chance to stay in the hole.

Everybody around the green knew what was happening. ESPN had come out and caught the last few holes. They caught the 17th hole, which was really an amazing birdie because the wind was coming right to left, the pin was on the right side of the green, and it was in between clubs again. I had to bank the ball off the edge of the green and bounce it into the green to give myself even a decent putt to try. The shot came off just right, bounced off the side of the green, and bounced up near the hole. Still, I had a tough curving right-to-left putt to make. When that putt fell, it was just amazing—whenever you make a 10- or 15-footer for birdie when you really *have* to make it, it feels almost like a miracle.

When I look back on it, I realize that on every hole I just gave myself a good chance, and things fell for me. That was the thing—just giving myself the chance to make things happen. Of course you still have to make the shots. This time I had made them all, and it felt great.

Keeping Cool

Coming up to the tee box on 18 with a chance to make birdie and shoot a 59 is perhaps more pressure than most golfers encounter in their careers. But because of the nature of the game, every serious golfer has probably played under pressure at some point. Some golfers thrive on pressure, and some have a hard time with it. Part of the difference is genetic makeup—some people seem to have ice water in their veins, and clutch situations bring out their best. It's also quite common, though, for golfers to "choke" under pressure. In this chapter we'll discuss key principles that can help even the shakiest golfers deal with pressure.

KEY PRINCIPLE: COPING SKILLS

Playing golf in highly pressurized situations requires the same coping skills that are helpful for handling other kinds of pressures. These coping skills help prevent choking and slumping and can help you in breaking out of a slump.

Whether you're performing in a boardroom, on the final exam, or out of the bunker, the skills that psychologists and other scientists have developed to help people handle stress and cope with adversity greatly help a golfer handle the many difficulties that occur, and the mounting pressure of playing a round in competition. Earlier we discussed learning good relaxation and mood-management skills, and these skills are even more important when you're in a high-stress or pressurized situation. Also, we have talked about the tremendous value that it is for golfers to learn strong imagery skills and practice visualizing what they are about to do. These skills are even more important when playing to win the tournament or under other high-pressure circumstances. Regarding performance under pressure, it's important to realize that the skills you've been learning to use for playing golf generally are even more important to have available for use under high-pressure situations.

There are also character traits that greatly help a person manage stress and handle pressure, and these are a subset of the cluster of attributes and skills that have recently come more into focus and have fallen loosely under the label of "emotional intelligence." These traits, which we will discuss in some detail shortly, are in fact skills that can be learned or enhanced. Once learned, they greatly help you avoid adversity, cope with it when it does occur, take things in stride, put things behind you, and move on to continue pursuit of golf improvement or other goals. Without high emotional intelligence, players become lost when the pressure mounts. They tend to fall apart and see a chance to win or make the cut disappear as their game vanishes under the pressure.

Choking and slumping are key problems in golf. There are specific techniques to help a player avoid choking and slumping, and skills that assist a player in breaking out of the slump when it occasionally happens. It's important for all players to realize that going into a slump is unavoidable at some time in their careers, and that peaks and valleys in one's game are going to occur no matter who you are or at what level you play. Whereas development of significant "antichoking" skills have the potential to eliminate chokes completely, it doesn't work quite that way with slumps. Slumps *will* happen, and the best you can do is reduce their frequency, depth, and duration, Developing the patience and emotional strength to ride out your slumps will take you a long way toward elevating your game and make it consistent, day in and day out.

In the next section, we'll suggest prescriptions to help handle elevated pressure on the course and the rising pressures between rounds of a tournament. Then we'll suggest ways to help avoid chokes and slumps, and to reduce the latter when they occur.

Pressure on the Ryder Cup

Mark Calcavecchia

The Ryder Cup is unlike any other thing you'll play in the field of golf. Yes, it's intense. I've been on a losing team, I've been on a tied team, and I've been on a winning team. Unfortunately, the year we tied, they won the year before, so we didn't get the Cup back, so it was just as bad as a loss. But I've been on both ends of the scale, the up and down end, and it's hard, to say the least. It's just a different kind of pressure. Maybe I put too much pressure on myself, but I think the other guys do, too, and I think everyone feels it. I guess that's what makes that competition so interesting—that you're playing for your country, and there's just ultimate pressure.

Not only are you playing for your country, but you've got a lot of other teammates and their families to think about, too. It's not just about *your* money and *your* pride anymore. It's like one great big group, with maybe 30 or 40 people involved, and you don't want to let them all down. You don't want anything to be your fault, so the pressure is really on. And, you know, the fact that you're playing for your country . . . well, it's gotten to be such a big deal that it's pretty intense out there. I can really understand why some guys can't stand the pressure and decline their chance to play on the Ryder. But that's a real shame because there's nothing else quite like it.

COPING SKILLS PRESCRIPTION

- Dismiss bad breaks
- Practice desensitization
- Understand choking to overcome slumps
- Focus on the positive

Pressure builds on a player in many different ways. Sometimes it builds because we find that we are playing poorly without any explanation for it. At other times it is because we feel that we have hit numerous good putts yet they keep "rimming out" and because of it our scores don't reflect our play. Pressure can build because a great drive off the tee lands in a middle of a fairway—but in a deep divot. Or pressure builds because of the "rub of the green" or because we so badly want to beat that "show-off" that we're playing against.

Dismiss Bad Breaks

Any of the above situations and hundreds more that you could describe happen to each of us who play golf virtually every round. If you're not to let pressure build that comes from getting angry about the unfair things that happen to you, you must learn to dismiss bad breaks. Several times a round you will get a bad break of some sort, and most players deep down feel that they get more than their share. Some tour players feel that they almost always get the bad weather, whether they play the late Thursday/early Friday sequence, or the early/late sequence in the first two rounds of the tournament. A tendency to notice the bad breaks more than the good ones is one of the elements of a negative mindset and low self-confidence. You need to practice techniques that allow you to dismiss bad breaks without letting them break your concentration and interfere with your ability to play the remainder of the hole or round. Dismissing bad breaks—to be able to let them go and move on—is critical to performing under pressure, because failing to do so adds to whatever pressure is already present, making it even more difficult to perform.

Along with bad breaks, you also want to dismiss your mistakes and other distractions over which you have no control. Thus, building the skill of dismissing the negatives that happen is critical to playing under pressure.

Practice Desensitization

A somewhat more sophisticated concept is the use of *desensitization* for bad breaks and mistakes and other adversities. Although somewhat more complicated to learn and carry out, desensitization has even greater potential for helping us keep pressure from building because it eliminates our negative reactions and overreactions to what occurs on and off the golf course. Desensitization involves the neutralizing of stimuli that produce negative reactions in us by replacing the negative reaction that has followed the stimuli with a positive reaction, such as a relaxation response. If, for example, missing an easy putt to go one down in your match previously produced an anger response as well as a fear of losing the match, following the missed putt with a successful relaxation response can very likely eliminate the anger and fear of losing. Desensitization reinforces skills that you have been building throughout this book—imagery, energy management, and relaxation responses. We'll lay out a useful desensitization skill-learning technique in the next section.

Understand Choking

Choking can be understood, recognized for what it is, and virtually eliminated through the use of techniques that help us avoid the critical choke that many players so greatly fear and which all too often begins performance on a steady downward decline.

A good working definition of choke is a dramatic decline or disruption of performance, often at the critical moment where success or failure is decided. Choking results from any one or several of the following: a rapid anxiety increase or other mood change (e.g., anger) that interferes with automatic execution of actions that are within our capacity and repertoire; intrusion of "right-brain" negative images (e.g., seeing oneself missing the putt) and/or "left-brain" negative self-talk (e.g., I'm going to miss the putt); failure to remain in the "present tense" with drifts into the past with negative experiences, into the future with worries about upcoming, more difficult events, and/or worries if performance can be maintained; and from self-blame from failure to accept performance interference when extraordinary external conditions or events occur.

In and of itself, choking can ruin a hole or a round, but making the situation worse is that we come to fear a "choke" that might come in the future, and this type of anticipatory fear makes the future choke more likely to happen. To fight this problem, we will outline several choke prevention maneuvers that you can learn to reduce the likelihood of choking and having it disrupt your whole round, your whole week, or even your whole summer.

A slump can be defined as a sudden fall in activity or performance below one's capacity and practiced skill level. Some slumps are short-lived and others can last many weeks or even months. There are two primary causes for slumps. The first involves problems with mechanics, health, practice routines, mental routines, or overall preparation for play, and the second involves the natural ebb and flow of performance through an athlete's normal performance range. This last type of slump is the only kind that requires no intervention. You need only the patience to do nothing different and to trust your experience and routines. After a while, the performance variance shifts back toward the middle of your performance range where it remains the majority of the time.

Focus on the Positive

Both negative and positive events are going to happen during a round and over a career, so you'll be doing yourself (and your spouse and family!) a favor if you learn to focus on the positive events and skip the negative ones. But similar to the way some people will dwell on the B on a report card rather than on the four As that accompany it, some golfers just can't get past the negative—even when there's much to be positive about.

Chip is known on the PGA tour as one of the players best able to focus on the positive. One television announcer said of Chip during a tournament in 1997, "He could find something positive in his dog dying." Well, Chip might dispute that, but it remains true that he's trained himself to get past the negative for a better, closer look at the positives, both in his golf career and his life. While a positive attitude won't fix everything, it is critical for reducing pressure and performing well under stressful circumstances.

In the same way that you might prepare for difficult times by practicing desensitizing and dismissing, you should also prepare for the good times, the peak moments where something so positive happens that it disrupts you and causes pressure. For example, Ken Doherty, a PGA member, was playing in a 36-hole one-day tournament in September, 1996, in St. Lucie, Florida. Up until that point in the year he had been having an average year playing and scoring, and his first round began similarly. However, he holed out a wedge for an eagle on 4, hit a 33-footer for birdie, birdied number 9, and played the back nine similarly for a 68 on the first 18. At this point Ken was surprising himself by leading the tournament.

That Ken wasn't comfortable leading the tournament was clear in that as he began to prepare for the second 18, he knew that at some point he was "going to get his game back" (i.e., come back down to earth and play at his expected level). Ken began the second 18 as he had the first, pulling birdies out of the air. Soon Ken was seven under, and he and his playing partners were in shock and laughing about how well he was scoring. "Everything I touched turned to gold," he recalls.

After knocking in a 15-footer on 5, Ken was at eight under, and his mind began to jump ahead. "I started thinking about the newspaper the next day, the money I was going to make, and so on." Ken was starting to feel uncomfortable because he had never been eight under, he was out of his "comfort zone," and when asked he stated that he didn't feel that he was "that good." He then began expecting that he would start bogeying and double bogeying at any time and "level out his play." Sure enough, two three-putts led to two double bogies and a final 36-hole score of around par. (Ken did hold on to finish a respectable fifth in the tournament.)

The unexpected lucky bounce that turns what would have been a difficult up and down for par into a birdie can be disruptive and can produce a "high" that becomes pressure to "keep it going." It's important to practice anticipating such good fortune so that on those rare occasions when it does occur, it is not disruptive. Ideally, such occasions should be built upon to continue good play, but it takes a golfer with strong mental skills to accomplish this.

Keep It Fun

Golf should be fun. If it's not fun, you'll have a much harder time reaching your performance goals. How many times have you heard an athlete explain quitting competition because "it just wasn't fun anymore"? Often the problem is burnout, but sometimes (including some cases attributed to burnout) it comes down to neglect. Athletes neglect to appreciate the reasons they got into the sport in the first place. After weeks of intense competition, or after a prolonged slump, they feel an incredible pressure to perform well, and this pressure sucks the enjoyment out of their sport or activity. To have fun again, they have to get back to their roots and remember how enjoyable the sport was back when it was just a game. That's the way to play golf—as if it's a game. When it becomes a chore, every bad shot is magnified and every good shot overlooked. On the other hand, when you're enjoying the game, you marvel at the beauty of your good shots and shrug at and forget the bad ones. It's not hard to figure out which attitude yields the better golf game.

Taking the Pressure Off

As we already stated, pressure-relieving techniques can be divided into two types: (1) the techniques that minimize the effects of various negatives, including bad breaks, mistakes, or collapses in your mental game or mechanics; and (2) techniques that involve benefiting from positives that occur, whether through luck or skill. Practice in each of these techniques can make for a powerful repertoire of weapons for withstanding pressure.

When practicing dismissing the negative, your techniques can be based in either imagery or self-talk, or be a combination of the two. They can also include dismissing negative *behaviors* as well as thoughts. Remember, too, that pressure itself can be conceptualized either as an image or as a topic for positive self-talk, and for maximum benefit you should probably practice desensitizing yourself to pressure directly. Some of our favorite images involve physically brushing off a bad break as you would brush lint off a jacket, encapsulating yourself in your own cocoon or suit of armor, throwing a bad shot away in the trash, or walking away from a bad hole, never looking back after it has been completed. Self-talk techniques involve suggestions that you are immune to pressure, that pressure rolls off you like rain off a raincoat. You are only limited by your own creativity in terms of coming up with statements and/or images that you can rehearse repeatedly so that they can be remembered easily when needed and trigger the self-protective mechanisms within you. For these techniques to have benefit, they should be practiced for at least several five- to ten-minute periods a day, and they are probably most helpful when used along with the somewhat more complicated desensitization techniques.

Pour on the Pressure

The classic desensitization procedure that psychologists use on fears and phobias can be directly applied on the golf course. First, create several scenes of events on the golf course that have resulted in your feeling mounting pressure to perform. Describe these scenes in as much detail as you can. Next, rank the scenes in the order of least pressure felt to most pressure felt. The scenes that evoke less pressure are the best to begin with when carrying out desensitization exercises. For each event or situation on your list, play the imagined scene in your mind at the same time you're maintaining a relaxed state that you produced for this purpose; try to maintain the relaxation as you run through the entire scene. Each time you successfully maintain the relaxed state in the face of the previous pressure-producing image, the imagined event loses some of its ability to trigger the negative and problematic responses. It might take several repetitions to neutralize the pressure-producing effects of the scene, but once it is neutralized proceed to the next scene in your ranking, working from the bottom toward the top in terms of degree of pressure experienced. After many days and weeks of this practice, you'll be much more ready to surmount pressure in all the situations you've practiced. As you become more adept at desensitizing, the process takes fewer repetitions to neutralize an event.

After you've succeeded in neutralizing your list of high-pressure scenes, you're in position to try what we call "in vivo" desensitization, which is to put yourself in the pressurized situation on the golf course and attempt to maintain the relaxation response while playing out the scene.

You can use this desensitization technique to reduce the effects of pressure on you, the effects of a poor shot or round, and on the negative tactics that some players use to attempt to upset or frustrate other players into poor play. If you read *Raising a Tiger*, the book written by Tiger Woods' father, you may recall how they used in vivo desensitization and dismissal techniques to help immunize Tiger to negative tactics and other pressures. Apparently, the techniques work as Tiger is one of the most mentally tough players on the tour.

Take It in Stride

Devalue the negative. Without deluding yourself, it's helpful to remind yourself how insignificant or unimportant a negative event is in the broader scheme of your game, your day, and your life. When you're in a slump or feeling low in self-confidence, it's easy to blow minor setbacks out of proportion (an activity we call *catastrophizing*). Yes, it's healthy to recognize and acknowledge where you are and what you're going through, but it's unhealthy and unreasonable to believe that you're stuck there. Catastrophizing can lead to complacency because you come to believe that no matter what you do things will end poorly for you. This unhealthy attitude amounts to feeling sorry for yourself and yields no gains whatsoever. To cultivate the attitude that best brings success, it's important to overcome the tendency to inflate the negative. Imaging exercises and focusing on the insignificance of negative events are perhaps the best ways to combat catastrophizing.

Focus on the execution of your skills and game as opposed to outcome. When you're focusing on such goals as achieving the swing that you desire or making a pre-shot routine automatic, you're working on factors within your control. If you focus on such things as improving your score and winning, you're reaching for goals that may be beyond your control. Focusing on creating and developing your game and technique will always increase your opportunity for satisfaction from your game, and it will often improve outcome as well.

Regular review of everything that is positive that happened in today's round, yesterday's round, or in last week's round begins to sink in and convince you that good will happen in the future because good has happened in the past. Focusing on past positives combines with the confidence-building exercises discussed in chapter 3 to help build strength and immunity to pressure.

Games Within the Game

Another positive technique is called "playing games within the game." When you're trying to distract yourself from the pressure of your score or place, it helps to create a different game in your mind—a game with different rules to take some of the pressure off. One of these games we call the one-good-stroke-per-hole game. In this game your goal is to hit one good shot per hole. All shots on the hole after the good shot are superfluous in this game, so the remainder of the hole can be played under less pressure. In the one-good-shot game you can have a perfect score of 18, having hit at least one good shot on each hole. As you get better, the game can be changed to two good shots per hole.

Like dismissing and desensitization, these focusing-on-the-positive exercises require practice to be successful. If you work on them on a regular basis, they can produce huge benefits in your ability to resist pressure and perform under the most difficult conditions.

We end this chapter with a worksheet for you to use with some of the techniques we've described here. With regular practice of these exercises, you'll be ready for most pressure situations you encounter on the course.

Figure 6.1 PERFORMING UNDER PRESSURE WORKSHEET

Days/Carried out procedure

Emotional control procedures	M	TU	W	TH	F	SA	SU
Relaxation							
Imagery							
Self-talk							
Dismissing							
Desensitization							
Anti-choke							
Focus on the positive							
Keep it fun							
Pour on pressure							
Take off pressure							
Games within the game							

Criteria: Pressure procedure carried out = Yes ; not carried out = No

Reward criteria: Pressure procedure carried out _____ times over _____ (days, weeks, etc.)

Reward: _____

chapter 7

Thriving on Competition

Competitive Fire

Ben Crenshaw

I've gotten better through the years. I used to be pretty volatile, *very* volatile, and I was my own worst enemy for a long time. I know losing my cool cost me some tournaments. I have a decent record, but I know my record could be better. We all know how important the mental faculties of golf are and how emotional the game is. I do believe that some of the best players were born with a tumultuous temper and they overcame it to make it work for them. The finest example I could give is Bobby Jones. He had a very volatile temper, an explosive temper,  and he was really tough on himself. If you divide his career into two halves—the seven fat years and the seven lean years—Bobby went a long time favored to win big tournaments. I mean, at a very young age, that's how good he was, and he was expected to win—but he didn't, and then he was very explosive. However, from the time he was about 21, 22, 23 on, he was a total model of control. He made his emotions and temperament work for him in a dramatic way. He was still burning with competitiveness, but he learned to channel that burn into a sharp focus. He blossomed and became one of the most gentlemanly golfers there's ever been—but he still had that competitive fire, you could tell.

Sam Sneed always said, "You show me a young person who has a little fire in his belly, and I'll show you somebody who might be a champion." You can't be complacent and get anywhere. Otherwise you wouldn't be perceived to have any inner drive. I'm not saying that there's a license for any kind of ill behavior, but if you have sort of a tempestuous view and you can learn about the game and its nature and what it does and how you can bottle those desires, then it tends to be a positive. For any person who is to achieve anything in life, you have to have an extremely competitive nature, I think. It may come to you over time. You can't just throw out a sweeping generalization and say, "Well, he's finally learning how to mature," or something like that. It's a little finer than that. It has more to do with learning to adjust your emotions than it does with maturing, I think. We all mature in different ways, but only

some of us learn how to use our big emotions to our advantage. This lesson proved to be a winning formula for Bobby Jones.

Competitive Spirit

To get away from golf for a moment, do you remember the fifth game of the 1997 NBA finals between the Chicago Bulls and Utah Jazz? Who could have watched that critical fifth game in Utah and not been in awe at the competitiveness of Michael Jordan? We saw someone too sick to play—too sick to be out of bed, really—refuse to give in to illness, refuse to recognize that the Bulls could still win the title if they lost the game by winning two on their home court in Chicago, and refuse to collapse when every message his body gave him was to stop and rest. The less-reported but most tell-tale part of the story was that Jordan had pushed himself over the edge and was almost catatonic in the locker room for 20 minutes after the game.

In a similar vein, when listening to PGA tour players talk about their desire to be in competition and in a position to win on Sunday, with many of them it's clear that you're hearing a burning desire, not just a preference. No matter what your sport or pursuit it's the competitors who get to the finish line most often. In golf, the kind of competitive spirit you see in Michael Jordan might be a little more beneath the surface, but it's there. You see it in players like Tiger Woods, the determination in his eye. It's true that in golf the laid-back approach seems to suit some professionals very well, but when it's crunch time on Sunday a strong streak of competitive spirit comes in mighty handy.

KEY PRINCIPLE: COMPETITIVENESS

You want a level of competitiveness that motivates you to develop your skills, gets you to practice regularly, and inspires you to put in the time to prepare to play well. You must develop, prepare, and overlearn all the components of your game, and then you must execute them to be in a position to remain competitive and win.

That competitiveness would be important for playing good golf is no surprise, but some people are surprised that a degree of competitiveness is equally important for golf to be satisfying. There are few people who really enjoy going out and playing a round of golf by themselves every day. A large part of the attraction of golf for most players is to go out with a group of buddies to play a game that is both friendly and competitive. There are probably more friendly wagers among friends during a round of golf than in any other sport.

Preparing to Win

A strong will to win is important, but what's crucial is a strong will to *prepare* to win. The best prepared golfers are usually the ones leading at the end of a tournament—and if they are in competition at the end of a tournament they have given themselves the best opportunity for good things to happen. Being the best prepared golfer means that when the game's on the line you're the most able to draw on your game plan, mechanics, and pre-shot and other routines to give you the edge over the other players remaining. Even the players who seem at first glance to be exceptions to the rules—those who seem to win because of their strong will—

probably owe a lot of their success to good preparation habits. Nick Faldo comes to mind in golf. Greg Maddux, Roger Clemons, and Tony Gwynn come to mind in baseball. Bobby Knight, the famous (or infamous) coach of the Indiana Hoosiers is perhaps the strongest proponent of the importance of developing a will to prepare to win. He refers constantly to the importance of being better prepared than his opponents. And the way Indiana prepares is to always try to improve on the execution of their own game rather than trying to change their playing style against different opponents.

Overlearn Your Game

The success of Coach Knight's philosophy on competitiveness and positioning his team to win cannot be disputed. Despite our disappointment with some of his personal behavior, his approach to preparing players to play their best fits right in with our views: you must develop, prepare, and overlearn all of the necessary components of your game, and then execute it to be in a position to win.

PGA tour players refer to the need to put all parts of their game in place in order to win big tournaments. They talk about needing to develop swing mechanics to compete at the level of competition in which they're playing. Then they point to the necessity of developing an adequate shot repertoire, again in order to compete. Next, they discuss the need to develop experience in competition and a history of winning at the elite level they play in. Once players have these four elements going for them, they talk about developing a winning strategy for competing in their tournaments. Then, finally, they get to the last ingredient of winning, a necessary but not sufficient one—*a winning attitude.*

THE SIX ESSENTIALS TO WINNING ON TOUR

1. *Proper swing mechanics*
2. *Adequate shot repertoire*
3. *Experience in competition*
4. *A history of winning*
5. *A winning strategy*
6. *A winning attitude*

Players need to constantly grow in each of these six areas if they are to advance far in professional golf. The areas do not develop at the same rate, and development in some of the areas more than others can be expedited with extra attention and extra practice. However, if any one of the six areas lags significantly behind the others in development, success at the pro level is unlikely if not impossible. When one of the areas of preparation is lacking, it's also unlikely for a player to succeed in moving to the next higher level of competition.

We have named the key principles or skills necessary to be in competition, thrive on competition, and put yourself in a position to win. The following prescriptions can help you develop the desire to be in competition, gain a competitive edge, and position yourself to win tournaments at whatever skill and competition level you have reached.

COMPETITIVENESS PRESCRIPTION

- Expose yourself to competitive situations
- Practice your routines, such as the GUIDES and CHECKS
- Play *your* game

Psychologists who study how people learn recognize that something we learn in one setting may not necessarily be available to us in another setting. This is an example of "state-dependent learning," which means that you'll best learn something and remember it in the situation or circumstances in which it was learned. You will have learned it much less well, and remember it less well, in situations or circumstances quite different from where it was learned. In situations *similar* to the original conditions, some of the learning will be evident, but not as much as in the original setting. Another way of saying this is that there is a gradient of ideal learning and retention, with less learning available as you move farther away from the situations and circumstances of the original learning.

This principle applies directly to performance in golf. For instance, if all of your learning and practice at driving occurs on the practice range, you'll have learned a behavior that works best on your particular practice range, somewhat less well on other practice ranges, less well yet at the tee boxes on your favorite course, and not well at all on tee boxes at a course you've never played. The principle also applies to chipping and putting and to your mental game, including your pre-shot routine. If, for instance, you only practice your pre-shot routine in your basement, or on the first ball that you hit at the driving range, then you'll have developed a pre-shot routine that has little relevance to, or benefit for, your game on the course. We want to emphasize this last example, as we see a significant mistake made by most players concerning their practice and preparation.

Try this yourself the next time you go to the driving range. Before you start to hit balls, watch several players for a few minutes to see how many of them use their pre-shot routine before every ball struck on the practice range. Most often you'll see either no shot routine or a shot routine used only before the first ball hit, or perhaps the first one hit with each club. After that, most players just pick up the next ball, place it on the tee, and whack it with no sign of their pre-shot routine. This pattern of practice results in most of the practice involving a shot that the player will never hit on the course—that is, a shot without a pre-shot routine. Thus, many players spend most of their practice time hitting a shot that is unlike the shots they will hit on the course and in competition. How much sense does that make? Not much. You may as well practice your putting with your five iron.

We suggest that you buy a small bucket rather than a big bucket of balls for the practice tee, that you stretch and warm up without hitting any balls, that you practice your swing without hitting balls, and that when you're ready to hit balls you use your pre-shot routine with *every* ball you hit. Quality practice beats quantity practice every time.

Two Types of Competitive Fire

Chip Beck

It's well known on the PGA tour that some players use gamesmanship and other means to try to distract or rattle fellow competitors to gain an advantage. The frequent "cough" of one European Ryder Cup player during the pre-shot routine and even the backswing of his American competitors brings to the surface an important issue in golf: Is it better for a golfer to remain cool, calm, and collected, to relax and just let his game speak for itself, or should he stalk his prey like a hunter and with a killer instinct attack the course and attempt to vanquish his opponents? The latter style runs smack

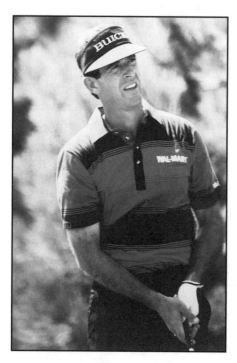

in the face of the picture of the gentlemanly golfer, of the sport that allows participants largely to govern themselves, where players are expected to turn themselves in, even for potential disqualification, when they realize a mistake that others might not have noticed. There are certainly many golfers on the tour who fit the first description, and there are many others who better fit the second. The question is, then, is one style or approach more competitive? Does one style have an advantage over the other?

There have been only a few incidents where I have become involved in a competitive situation with another player, and on most of these occasions, a competitive fire has been ignited only when I've felt another player has treated me in an unsportsmanlike manner. Otherwise, I try to let the behavior of other players wash off me.

Karen, my wife, has summed it up this way: "Chip knows the intimidation tactics of certain players, and he finds them amusing. Chip says it's like a guy who digs the hole is the first to fall into it. Intimidation factors mainly show the weakness in the player who's trying to be intimidating."

It's true that I don't play the games that a lot of players try to bring me into playing. I think that some players use intimidation as a tool, a form of competition, like another club in their bag to beat you, and I always find that funny. It's difficult to deal with when you're early in your career, but as you get older and more mature, it's really humorous, and you understand that such behavior is self-defeating. As a veteran, and as you gain more wisdom and confidence in your ability, it's easier to recognize that the guy who throws the first stone is usually the one who gets smacked by it.

I look forward to good competition, and I recognize that for some these behaviors are a part of competition. They don't ruin the fun of the game for me. In fact, I think the high degree of competition is what has made the Ryder Cup so enjoyable for me—you know it's like going to war, but behind all that, it really is fun. You look forward to the competition and try to thrive on it. I think everybody knows that you need a competitive posture, as that is what makes you excel and become better than you would have been otherwise.

Expose Yourself to Competitive Situations

The discussion about state-dependent learning and our difficulty in transporting learning from one setting and circumstance to another illustrates the importance of exposing yourself to as many competitive situations as possible, during both practice and play, if you are to become a good competition player. Sign up for many tournaments—big tournaments, small tournaments, tournaments where you expect to do well, and others where you probably won't. It's important to pit yourself against excellent competition, and you should give yourself credit for doing so. No matter how well you play in the tournament, the experience of playing in elite competition will strengthen you and add to your playing experience—as long as you can dismiss your negative shots and not be discouraged. Second, set up friendly competitions when you play with your friends, as the more play you can experience with something on the line the more experience you'll have playing in competition and the tougher in competition you'll become. Third, set up games and competitions with yourself when you practice, such as needing to hit a certain percentage of chips to within 10 feet of the cup from a certain distance to earn yourself a reward. We'll say more about the details of such practice in the next section, but the point is that the more of this kind of competition you can experience, and the more competitive atmospheres you play in, the more your mind and body will desensitize to the conditions and the more you'll be able to execute the behaviors that you've learned in your competitive practice.

Practice Your Routines

Whenever you're attempting to learn a new skill that you wish to apply in competitive settings, we suggest you use the GUIDES we introduced in chapter 1: set goals involving performance in competitive settings; use the techniques for understanding and awareness in competitive settings; implement your learning program in competitive settings; carry out your disciplined practice in competitive settings; and evaluate and reward your performance in competitive settings. This way the maximal retention of your learning can occur and you can have maximal execution of this learning in the future. If you think back to chapter 1, you remember that the GUIDES are designed to create a process that allows for optimal learning of a new skill. Goal setting, as it applies to preparation for competitive play, involves deciding on how you're going to gradually expose yourself to more and more demanding competitive golf situations. You might begin with a simple goal of increasing the frequency of involvement in competitive play, such as raising the number of tournaments you play per month.

A second goal might be planning your tournament play schedule to include tournaments that are below your skill level. In these tournaments you may be in competition to win, and playing under that sort of pressure is good for you even if the competition is a little weak. You also should schedule some tournaments at your skill level, where your opponents have handicaps similar to yours and most of the players could be competitive. Third, you might schedule tournaments in which most of the players have lower handicaps than yours and you're not expected to compete to win. All three kinds of tournaments have much to offer in terms of helping you develop your mechanics, mental game, and competitive attitude and strategy and give you playing experience in competitive situations.

The competitive play goals should also include subgoals, such as what you wish to work on at each of the tournaments that you enter. For example, you might set goals concerning the number of fairways hit, greens hit in regulation, the percentage of "near-perfect matches" between imagined shot and executed shot, and the number of two-putt greens. It's best to have no more than two subgoals to work on for each tournament and to work on the same subgoals for several tournaments instead of making new ones for each outing.

You'll also want to apply the CHECKS, introduced in chapter 2, in competitive settings, scheduling several practice sessions using your confidence, health/physical, energy and emotion management, concentration, knowledge, and strategic routines to get maximum benefit under competitive conditions. When necessary, modify the CHECKS to better fit the demands and skills required during competitive play, and use them during and after competitive play to take advantage of what we know about state-dependent learning and difficulties in generalizing learned behavior from one situation to another. For instance, in practicing the procedures to increase your confidence, some of your imagery sessions succeeding at golf should involve your participating in various levels of competitive play. Thus, in addition to imagining effective ball striking on the practice range, you should imagine desired ball striking in a round with your friends with "something on the line," ball striking while playing in your club tournament, and effective ball striking in your club championship.

Concerning your body preparation routines, imagine carrying them out before and during competitive play, and actually do so before and during selected tournaments or other competitive play. Similarly, practice your energy and emotion management and concentration skill-building techniques before and during competitive play as well as imagining doing so (and imagining positive outcome from doing so) to allow these skills to be strongest and most easily accessed when in competitive settings.

Finally, knowledge/game plan and strategic routines should also be developed with competitive play in mind. There may be some differences in applying both knowledge and strategy when preparing for competitive versus recreational play. For instance, concerning game plan, you may choose to play more aggressively in recreational play than in competitive play, or, alternately, to play less aggressively in one aspect of your game in tournaments where you expect to be in competition with a good chance to win as opposed to tournaments where you have nothing to lose because of the superior skill level of the competition. Likewise, your game plan in recreational play may not even include efforts to shoot the lowest score but might involve working on some aspect of your game that requires you to take more strokes to complete your round (e.g., playing a round without using any woods). Using the CHECKS in this way should make them maximally beneficial in enhancing your readiness for competitive play as well as for helping you elevate your game under other types of conditions, such as recreational play or skill-development play.

Ryder Cup Competitiveness

Chip Beck

Most professional golfers played as part of a team in high school and college, but only the more successful ones get to experience team play within the tense competition of the Ryder Cup or President's Cup where players from one country or continent are pitted against those of another. These competitions are very spirited—in some countries fans are as fanatical about their golf team as they are about their soccer squad. Players recognize that it takes special mental and emotional talents to succeed under these high-pressure conditions. I've played on three Ryder Cup teams—1989, 1991, and 1993—and have found it to be an experience like no other.

I really hadn't thought much about the Ryder Cup before it started coming into prominence after the Americans lost it at Muirfield Village Golf Club in 1987, when Jack Nicklaus was captain at his own course. People really started hearing about it then. I played well in 1988 and wound up earning my way onto the next team as the second-highest point scorer behind Curtis Strange.

To give you an idea how tense Ryder Cup play was, even Tom Watson couldn't sleep the night before a match! Here was Tom, one of the few great champions, and he was tossing and turning like the rest of us. (For the record, Tom and I played Seve Ballesteros and Jose Maria Olazabal. The match ended in a draw.)

The Ryder Cup is the ultimate in competition because there's so much riding on it—especially for the European players, whose contracts sometimes hinge on the quality of their play in the Cup. When I teamed with Paul Azinger in 1989, our personalities really jelled well. Paul is loaded with talent, spunk, and tenacity, whereas I internalize more. Plus, we were both Ryder Cup rookies, so we had a similar amount of awe and respect to be among the participants. We were up against Ian Woosnam and Nick Faldo—two of the top five players in the world at the time. I remember Paul

and me watching as these guys holed-out from the bunker (twice!), chipping in and doing all kinds of spectacular things. But Paul and I played some tremendous golf that day and somehow managed to beat them.

At the Ryder Cup matches in 1991, I was a team choice at the Ocean Course at Kiawah Island, South Carolina. Our team won 14-1/2 to 13-1/2 in some of the highest drama you'll ever see on a golf course. I beat Ian Woosnam three and one in a big singles match the final day, but the Cup all came down to Bernard Langer's putt as the sun set on the final night. If he had made it, the Europeans would have retained the Cup by tying us. But Bernard missed—barely. I'll always remember his scream of anguish when the ball failed to drop in. (To Bernard's credit, he went home to Germany and won the following week. It was a real test of his character, as well as his skill.)

The fans go crazy at the Cup; they make noise the entire match and even clap at missed putts! That is just part of the competition there, the toughness of it. Initially, it was sort of strange and disconcerting, but after a while you begin to really enjoy it. Like Tom Watson told me, "Just play well and enjoy the silence."

The sense of purpose is so strong at the Ryder Cup that it carries over into the next tournament you play and you continue to thrive on competition. A perfect example was in 1991. Overcoming the disappointment of not playing as much as I wanted, I performed well against Woosnam on Sunday. Then I took a week off because I was so exhausted. My first week back on the tour, I shot my 59 at the Las Vegas.

Playing *Your* Game

Even during competition, you should set process goals rather than outcome goals. Although your desire to play well in competition is obviously going to be stronger than it is in recreational play, it's perhaps even more important to define goals that you can have complete control over, as opposed to focusing on outcome where so many factors are outside of your control. At first it seems paradoxical that focusing on process goals produces better outcome than outcome goals do directly, but the truth of this has been demonstrated many times. Initially, you may find it difficult to focus on hitting fairways and increasing your percentage of successful up and downs when you most want to be winning tournaments. Still, increasing your percentage of successful "matches" between actual shot execution and the constructed and imagined shot are the little successes that good scoring is made of—and this also results in overall positive outcomes in competition.

During competition also practice games within games, emphasizing execution over outcome goals, and playing your own game. If you want these attitudes and behaviors to be available in competitive contexts you need to work on them in such contexts. Yes, it's difficult to think about playing games within the game when you're in competition to win a tournament, but if you can focus, for instance, on playing a three-hole stretch of the course more effectively than you did the day before, this game within the game could result in good scoring in competition.

Finally, it's critical that you stay with your preparation, with hitting shots you have practiced and know you can hit, and to play your own game against your own talent and skill level instead of getting caught up in someone else's game or entering a personal competition with another player or group of players.

For many players, the allure of the game is the competition, whether it be personal competition with yourself, friendly competition with buddies on a Saturday afternoon, or the competition of the Nike tour, the LPGA, the Senior tour, or the PGA tour. Doing well in competition and sometimes even winning can be such an incredible high for most golfers that it can overshadow how enjoyable the game can be played competitively or recreationally at almost any level. Remember that to be successful at golf and improve your skills and your game, you need to be well-practiced and prepared to play *and* have a strong mental game that allows you to truly enjoy playing the game and be satisfied with your performance. We've seen so many golfers with such high potential who have fallen to the wayside because they burn out and cease to enjoy the game. The main secret to keep this from occurring is to do whatever it takes to enjoy the game. For most, though not all, golfers, enjoyment requires a competitive element. However, while thriving on competition, you also need to take care not to let it override your original goals and values.

chapter 8

Reviewing Your
Mental Scorecard

Winning in Golf . . . and in Life

Chip Beck

One thing that golf has taught me is how to deal with disappointment and "failure," how to cope with those things I haven't accomplished that I wish I would have by this point. Yes, for every one of my success stories, I have a "failure" story to go with it. But do I consider myself a failure? No way. Just as you can't elevate yourself and feel satisfied after you've won a tournament or two, neither can you diminish yourself because of some bad outings. If you start doing that, your enjoyment of the game disappears. And whether you're a golfer, a carpenter, a teacher, or an accountant, once the enjoyment for the "game" is gone, it's very difficult to "score" well.

Without a sense of inner peace and fulfillment, there's no way to be at your best in life. Have I found inner peace and fulfillment on the golf course? No. Have I been able to get past my disappointments, as well as my successes, and reach a point where I can find peace and fulfillment *off* the course? I think so. And can I carry this peace onto the course to help me through the bad times in my golf career? Well, I think I'm getting better at that.

In our crazy game, a player might swing like Ben Hogan and never make a cut. Another might swing like Hulk Hogan and win a tournament. Before you began reading this book, maybe you wondered how that could be. Now you know that the difference is the mental game. A really tough mental game will overcome many deficiencies. We've discussed that it takes hard work, commitment, and practice to develop a strong mental game. The other secret is no secret, really: you have to enjoy the game. If a delusion of failure or other circumstances in your life cause you to lose your basic love, enjoyment, or respect for the great game of golf, you'll never play the game as well again. On the other hand, if you combine hard work with reachable goals and a strong mental game, you will win often in your life, including on the golf course.

Stepping Back to Evaluate

One of the big changes occurring in our society, and in the entire industrialized world, is the increased need to evaluate virtually anything that we do. Our government, for example, has initiated "zero-based budgeting," where every program that applies for funding must be evaluated on whether it has met its goals and on whether the goals could be reached with less expense and greater efficiency. Likewise, the healthcare industry has been revolutionized by "managed care," the essence of which is the provision of timely, cost-effective, and proven services that have been studied and evaluated and demonstrated to be the best for the money.

On a national level, this trend toward evaluation is an attempt to make our activities more cost effective during a time of dwindling resources. On an individual level, people are getting more matter-of-fact and conscious of the bottom line, as evidenced by the familiar phrase of the late 1990s, "Show me the money!" We all want to know, or we are being forced to prove, that what we're doing has value. Put another way, we're becoming obsessed with whether or not what we think we're doing is in fact what we are doing, and whether or not it has any benefit.

Keeping It in Perspective

Bruce Lietzke

I had a grand life plan that was fairly clear to me all along except for some of the details, which depended mainly on my success on the golf course. I had a plan to play golf as a career, yet I also had dreams of being a father, being very active, and being a Little League coach.

The first part of my plan was to play golf. I also planned to hold off on getting married, or too emotionally tied down, in those first few years of touring. I purposely dated very little in my first four or five years on tour. Golf was my number one priority then and it really had been through adolescence, high school, and afterward. Yet again, I had those thoughts of being a husband and father, so I purposely steered away from emotional ties with women, both on tour and at home. During this period I hung around married couples all the time. My best friends were all married. My plan was still to play golf as hard as I could for a few years and put off everything else. Exactly how long I would play on the tour was still an unknown as I didn't know how successful I was going to be. I didn't know if I was going to lose my card or whatever. As it turned out, I had some success within a couple of years of getting my card, and everything stabilized pretty well.

I met my wife four or five years after I turned pro. We dated for a couple of years and, again, I was in no real hurry. My wife will confirm that I talked a lot about kids when we were dating, but I wasn't really convinced that I wanted to get married. However, we married in 1981, while golf was still my number one priority. My plan was becoming a little more focused by this time.

The biggest decision we had to make was when we would have our children. With no kids, my wife could travel with me, and there was no restriction on my golf. However, I knew there would be restriction once we had kids. So, the two of us decided to travel together for a couple of years before having kids.

The plan worked perfectly. We waited a couple of years and then had our kids exactly when we wanted them. I had decided long before that once the kids were born I was never going to play a full schedule with 28 or 30 tournaments again. The children did travel with us some, but I didn't believe that hotels were the place for kids to grow up, and I didn't want my wife to have to watch the kids alone while I was on the course. So, I cut back on golf and started playing in fewer tournaments.

In 1983, when my son was born, golf dropped from my number one priority to number five, behind my relationship with God, family obligations, my relationship with my wife, and my kids. Golf moved back behind these, and I've never had any regrets about it. I look at my career as two different golf careers—first the years when I did everything I could and measured myself against all the other guys. I knew exactly where I was on the money list every single week. I knew who was behind me and who was ahead of me. When the kids were born, the second part of my golf career started, and I'm equally as proud of this part. I'm proud to play as little as I do and still come out and be competitive at times. But I don't get the satisfaction from golf that I used to because it's not the most important thing. I get more satisfaction from being with my wife and kids and enjoying my relationships with them. In these things I'm probably more successful than in my golf career. I have a wonderful marriage and a terrific relationship with my kids—these are the most important to me now.

KEY PRINCIPLE: EVALUATION

For change in any process to occur, you need to thoughtfully and systematically evaluate your progress toward your stated goals.

For our purposes, to *evaluate* means to determine the progress toward a goal and the benefits of a program. To evaluate our program and our progress within it means we have to develop a system of evaluation that allows us to accurately determine cause and effect—if what we're doing in fact causes the outcome that we desire. Thus, to make gains in our golf game, we must set up thoughtful, reachable goals and develop a systematic, concrete program for reaching those goals. We have already done this earlier in chapter 1, where we discussed the GUIDES for change.

The Five Rs of Evaluation

Even if you choose to use the GUIDES as your program for change, you'll still need a systematic, organized method for evaluating the program. If you don't, you'll be lost in confusion about what you're doing and whether it has any benefit. An evaluation program will inform you on the success of your performance-enhancement program. We've labeled our evaluation program "the five Rs," which stand for review, reward, re-evaluate, rework, and re-execute.

EVALUATION PRESCRIPTION

• *Apply the five Rs—Review, Reward, Re-evaluate, Rework, and Re-execute—to make sure you're working toward the goals you want to achieve*

The first R, *review*, involves looking back over your collected data or your written summary of scores and deciding whether you were successful at accomplishing the goal as it was originally set up. If so, and if you met the criteria for reward—the second R—you must not fail to reward yourself in the established way to motivate yourself to continue working toward your goals. If you did not accomplish the goal and did not earn a reward, the third R comes into play, where you re-evaluate your program to determine why it was unsuccessful. You then need to rework the program to give yourself a better chance of success. Finally, you're in position to re-execute the program which brings you back to the beginning and the opportunity for review and reward.

The combination of the GUIDES to construct a change program and the five Rs to review the program is all you really need to maximize your chances of producing positive performance change for yourself in golf or any other life activity. In the next section, we'll prescribe the use of the five Rs for evaluating your program and your progress at several points in your golf season and during the off-season.

18 Pars

Hale Irwin

If someone were to ask me about my philosophy of play, I might say, "I've always felt that 18 pars is a good target to aim for. No one can knock 18 pars." Overall, that's a pretty good score, even in today's game. Years ago it would have been fantastic. Seventy-two pars on this golf course—you'll be surprised what you can make, although you won't win.

If you eliminate some of the high scores, you have the opportunity for low scores. That's all I'm ever trying to do is to get myself in position to win on the last nine holes. I'm not trying to win or lose on one hole. I aim for par, and if something better happens, hey, that's fine.

Setting Up the Holes

Mike Reid

I think that many people simply look at a scorecard in terms of the front nine and back nine. You'll even hear amateurs say, "Boy, that front nine chewed me up, but I can do better on the back nine." They'll divide the course up the way the card divides it up. That's very seldom the way courses are actually laid out as far as strategy of either the architect or the way it plays. It's a series of 4- or 5-hole sets, and sometimes 2-hole sets. That's the way I try to gear it. I try to look at the course and break it down into five or six 2- to 5-hole sets. That's the way I form my strategy during my preparation.

Applying the Five Rs

We've talked about the changes that you're trying to make when you practice, such as improvements in your concentration or energy level or in your pre-shot routine. The five Rs should be used after your practice. First, you review your efforts; then you reward yourself if you've reached a goal or subgoal. You should continually re-evaluate your program, reworking it to make it more effective in bringing about your desired changes. Finally, you want to re-execute the program, doing it over and over again, as successful repetition of your change activities brings about lasting change and improvement.

You can also use the five Rs after a round to gain full benefit from the round. First, review your efforts—how well you dismissed bad shots, stayed in the present, and raised or lowered your energy level as needed. Next, reward your effort for motivation, and then re-evaluate how you went about playing your round, prepared for it, made your decisions during it, and reacted to how it went. Next, if necessary, rework your strategy and preparation (and possibly even your attitude and motivation) as you prepare for the next competition. Finally, and only after you've done all the other steps, attempt to re-execute the golf game you have always dreamed about.

18 Holes of Growth

Throughout this book we have emphasized that the best golf is consistently played by the best-prepared player. We have also stressed that being well prepared means that you have developed positive mental and physical skills that allow for good golf performance, and that you have developed thoughtful routines for physical conditioning, practicing, and executing skills.

In what follows, we have summarized 18 of the most important issues, principles, and techniques covered in this book. We refer to them as "growth holes" because if you learn and use at least some of them regularly your golf game will grow, as will your satisfaction and enjoyment of the game.

These growth holes relate to skills, attitudes, and actions that apply not just to golf but to many life areas, and to play them means to give yourself a tremendous opportunity to grow in many ways. After we play these 18 holes, we'll conclude this round of our discussion with our 19th Hole, which is our individual views on golf and why it is *the* game of growth for all age groups and for any player from 8 to 80.

Hole #1—*To improve your golf, you must be motivated enough to work at improving.* You should develop a step-by-step change program to move toward improvement. You need patience enough to stay with the program until it pays off.

Hole #2 —*To ease your efforts at improving your game, use the GUIDES for behavior change.* Begin by setting realistic and objective goals. Make yourself aware of where you're starting from and understand clearly what you're trying to accomplish. Implement your program and carry it out with disciplined practice. Evaluate your progress and efforts, and when you succeed or show progress, reward yourself to get satisfaction and motivate yourself to continue.

Hole #3—*Preparation routines, thoughtfully constructed and regularly practiced, govern, control, and automate behavior.* They produce improved performance that helps overcome choking and slumping. Develop routines for precompetition, pre-shot, post-shot, and post-round to take full advantage of your practice and performance.

Hole #4—*Before competition, use the CHECKS.* This will allow you to gauge your confidence level, your health and physical preparation for play, your energy level and emotional state, your concentration, and your knowledge base. Review your strategies, including game plan and routines to prepare yourself for play. Check off each of the checks as you review them and strengthen them in preparation for play.

Hole #5—*Self-confidence is a learned skill that you can strengthen and make more consistent with regular practice.* Self-confidence can become a positive "habit" that supports your game and strengthens it in the face of adversities.

Hole #6—*Believe in your golf skills and expect success.* Trust your practice and preparation for play.

Hole #7—*Imagery and self-talk promote change and improve performance.* Mentally replaying past successes and rehearsing desired golf behaviors builds confidence in your golf and elevates performance.

Hole #8—*Physical conditioning, regular exercise, proper and sufficient stretching, and physical readiness to compete combine with your mechanics and your mental game to improve your golf performance.*

Hole #9—*Develop an ability to listen to and understand your body's messages.* Your body is constantly informing you about its status. Before you can control your physical arousal and tension levels for improved performance, you need to learn to listen to your body.

Hole #10—*Develop the skill of altering your physical arousal level.* Controlling your breathing patterns is one of the best ways to control and change your physical arousal levels.

Hole #11—*Develop awareness of and control over your emotional states.* Obsessiveness, perfectionism, and other potentially problematic mental and emotional states must be controlled for you to improve performance.

Hole #12—*Use thought stopping, dismissing, and desensitization techniques to reduce negative mental conditions and improve concentration and performance.* Replace the negative conditions with positive thoughts, prepared and practiced for this purpose.

Hole #13—*Stay in the present.* Focusing on what you can control, avoiding distractions, and automating routines all contribute to improved concentration and performance.

Hole #14—*Practice mental, emotional, and physical skills in imaginary and actual pressurized situations to improve your performance when playing under pressure.*

Hole #15—*Develop and use mental, emotional, and physical control techniques to reduce the frequency, intensity, and duration of choking and slumping.*

Hole #16—*Practice your mental, emotional, and physical skills during competitive practice and in competition to improve performance during competition.*

Hole #17—*Use the five Rs to evaluate and rework your golf change program.* This will increase the chances that you will achieve your improvement goals in the long run.

Hole #18—*Reward both effort and progress.* Remember to enjoy your efforts to become a better golfer, to be satisfied with the progress you make, and to have fun as you grow as a golfer.

The 19th Hole

More than three years have passed since Chip and I began to explore our joint feeling that golf might be unique among sports in its ability to teach character and growth issues. We wondered if these special properties were responsible for golf becoming part of the American psyche and synonymous with personal achievement. Golf is one of only a few sports (along with swimming and tennis) that can be played competitively and for pleasure through every life phase, from young child to senior citizen. As it's well known that many important business deals are cut on the links, golf is also the only sport that has become a part of the American business community. In fact, business people might be held back from advancement in their careers because they don't play golf or don't play it well enough to avoid "embarrassing" their company. Golf lessons are now as common in the United States as piano lessons or swimming lessons. Finally, golf has become a social lubricant that affords people an opportunity to begin conversation with others who have this interest (which borders on addiction) in common. What is it about this game that makes it the first response of many recently retired people when they're asked, "What are you going to do now?"

I've watched the tour and tour players with intense interest for the last three years and have given many group workshops on mental skills training in golf. I've worked with recreational, high school, college, and professional golfers to give them that extra mental lift that boosts their game to the next level. And over the years, from what I've seen, it seems to me that golf's unique attraction centers on its place as the most clear-cut example in sports of a personal quest for achievement uncontaminated by "team" issues. Perhaps one of the reasons for golf's hold on us is that no other game I can think of pays off as well in terms of progress and development as a result of hard work, discipline, and dedication to excel.

An 18-hole round of golf is a 4+ hour journey into a player's personality and into his or her needs, aspirations, defenses, and fantasies. As that player tours the 18 holes of the course, he or she is confronted with problems to solve, insights to discover, and unexpected challenges that will test ingenuity, creativity, and intelligence. The highs a golfer feels upon surmounting a course's challenges are extremely high, and the lows felt after a bad day on the course are extremely low.

At one level the game seems so easy—a stationary ball is hit by a stationary person with no one trying to block the shot or get in the way. Of course those who play the game know it is not at all easy. Still, the knowledge of its difficulty doesn't seem to reduce the sense of frustration, anger, and self-recrimination that occurs for many players when they do not perform up to their expectations. It also seems true for many that playing good golf is important enough to neutralize many negative things happening in the golfer's life.

As I've become more involved with golf and golfers, I've begun using golf analogies to explain psychological principles and to identify and analyze important aspects in my patients' lives. It has surprised me that these analogies seem to be more easily grasped and to register at a deeper level with most of my patients, even for those who don't play golf. Concepts such as frustration, anger, hope, trust, discipline, and character are quickly understood when put in the context of the golf course. As of yet, I have no explanation for this, but perhaps it has something to do with the eternal hope of golf. If you blow one hole, there's another right after it on which you can redeem yourself. If you blow that one, well you just move on to the next one. Indeed, golf addiction is easy to understand when you see the incredible positive reinforcement that occurs in someone who, after a day's worth of hooks and slices, hits just one good shot. I think as much as anything it's the look on that person's face that keeps me captivated by the game.

Four years ago, my wife and children knew nothing about the game of golf. Since then, they have come to see it as an amazingly intense emotional rollercoaster ride that goes on relentlessly for hours at a time. My wife has remarked that she can't imagine how anyone could engage in such a stressful sport, either for recreation or as a vocation. These are her feelings despite the fact that she is a forensic psychologist who evaluates criminals for a living and who comes face to face every day with some of the most painful, ugly, and stressful aspects of our society. Despite that background, or perhaps because of it, her impressions of golf as being more stressful than her career suggests that there's something truly fundamental about the personal struggle that the game seems to become for most people who take it up.

Finally, despite my 20 years in practice as a licensed clinical psychologist, and my several years as an interested and close hands-on observer of the game of golf, I honestly admit that the game has turned out to be at once both more simple and much more complicated than I had ever considered. Perhaps it is this last observation, of the co-existence in golf of a great simplicity and a great complexity that makes it so much like our lives in general. At first glance, our lives are simple. We have a few basic needs that must be met that we have inherited as part of our species. At one level all we need to do is work enough to earn enough money to feed, clothe, and shelter ourselves and our families, and if we succeed in accomplishing these, we have met the primary life tasks. However, once these needs are met, the complexity of life sets in as the myriad of "second-order" needs, our aspirations, wants and desires, and fears combine with the problems caused by our social and affiliative nature to produce anything but simplicity.

Golf's paradoxical simplicity and complexity and our need to both experience it and "solve" it seems to be made up of the very same elements that go into our need to do more in life than simply eat, stay alive, and procreate. I played some golf as a young boy. I played a little less in high school. Then from the time I was 18 until my twins were born when I was 36, I did not pick up another golf club. Since then, most of the golf I've played has been with my young children. Without their being told, and without their even having had the opportunity to observe the struggles that most feel playing golf, these young children have somehow developed a strong need to do well in this activity with an intensity of desire that is surprising, even in relation to their other needs, wants, and aspirations. Interestingly, the only other activities that seem to produce this same intense need in my children to acquire skills has been their desire to learn music and play musical instruments. It occurs to me that the basic need to play golf well in many ways resembles the need felt by some people to play music well, and it is widely recognized, although poorly understood, that music seems to touch a very primitive and fundamental chord in the human psyche. Maybe golf, too, strikes this chord.

The similarities between music and golf continue. Throughout history many musical geniuses have been considered obsessed or insane, and it certainly seems to be common to hear people say they are "crazy" about golf. Many people seem obsessed with playing golf, and they seem to get crazier about it than they get about almost anything else in their lives. Golf seems to be something that we as players are both crazy about and get crazy over, and clearly anything that has that kind of power and control over us must indeed be more than a game. Finally, maybe playing golf is more like playing music than it is like playing other sports because it's not really a sport at all. Perhaps golf is an art that we desperately keep trying to turn into a science with our new equipment technologies, our swing mechanics, and the like. Maybe it's also as much like dance as it is like music, and perhaps the people currently attempting to teach golf by first teaching rhythm and dance are on the right track.

Many movements and sounds that are smooth and rhythmic are both pleasing and comforting. People enjoy being at the beach watching waves rhythmically coming in and going out against the shoreline. The experience is heightened by the rhythmic sound of the water perfectly choreographed with the vision. Pleasant sounding metronomes tick at different speeds; pendulums of grandfather clocks peacefully pace back and forth; yoga and various hypnotic techniques are based on rhythmic movement or other responses; and rocking chairs and rocking infants calm us and them better than almost anything. We lie and swing in hammocks and swings, we sway to the beat, and we do "the wave." Finally, many of the most difficult activities in sports, the long "routines" of Olympic figure skaters and ice dancers, hitting a 95 mile-per-hour baseball, and even for some NBA players the "simple" free throw, all appear to be very difficult chains of behaviors that are poorly and awkwardly done until we find our rhythm.

The final statement is just a different way of saying what we have said before—that we do many complicated repetitive behaviors better when we stop thinking about what we're trying to perform. We let the right sides of our brains take over for the left sides. We go on autopilot and just let it happen.

For the sake of argument, let's say golf is more like art than sport, and more like dance and music than basketball or football. We know that these other art forms have been around for tens of thousands of years and that they have been for many peoples and cultures both a form of recreation and communication. Many people believe that dance and music are almost basic human needs. If so, maybe the desire to play golf well is just another expression of these needs, and thus it may be more basic than even most of us have thought. When I began this study I had a feeling that golf was more than a game. Chip Beck had the same feeling, so we embarked together on a golf-based journey of growth and discovery. What we found was an art form both simple and complex, one much more basic to our needs than even Chip and I could have ever guessed.

appendix

Imagery Relaxation Script

Lie back and get as comfortable as you can . . . relax to the best of your ability . . . just relax . . . let your body go limp . . . let your muscles relax . . . begin relaxing by taking three deep breaths from your stomach . . . inhale and fill your lungs . . . exhale . . . let the tension out of your body . . . three deep breaths in and out . . . that's fine . . . deep breaths . . . in and out . . . we are going to use a technique of tensing a few muscles and relaxing them to help us deepen . . . to help us deepen your level of relaxation . . . just for a moment tense up the muscles in your hands, arms, shoulders, and legs while holding your breath . . . tense them good and tight . . . fine . . . good and tight . . . then all at once relax . . . exhale . . . let your body go limp . . . let the muscles relax . . . let your body go limp . . . let your muscles relax . . . let the chair support your weight . . . muscles have nothing to do but relax . . . that's fine . . . now tense the muscles in your hands, arms, and legs all over again while holding your breath . . . then all at once exhale and release all the tension and let your body float . . . that's fine . . . let your body float . . . comfortably relaxed . . . that's fine . . . while relaxing like this, let go of all tension, letting feelings of discomfort or agitation drift away . . . let these feelings drift away as you allow your body to float . . . we can use the mind and its ability to imagine pleasant and relaxing things to help you relax even further, more relaxed than you are now . . . begin to focus your attention, your mind's eye, on the sound of my voice . . . allow your focusing on my voice and on the images I describe to you . . . let other extraneous noises and distractions drift off . . . off far away . . . outside of your consciousness . . . outside of your awareness . . . let them all go drifting away . . . now in this comfortable relaxing state I would like you to imagine that it's summertime, that you're lying on the beach . . . lying on the beach just kind of looking over the shoreline . . . watching the waves roll in . . . it's warm, pleasant . . . you can hear the sounds of summer in the background . . . listen to the waves as they roll in . . . let the waves move up and back on the shoreline . . . let the waves roll in . . . let the foam spread on the sand . . . and then the waves slowly begin to recede before starting again . . . this gentle rhythmic coming and going of the waves . . . gentle rhythmic motion back and forth . . . up and back of the waves . . . let this gentle relaxing motion take you down to a deeper state of relaxation . . . let it take you down to a deeper state of relaxation . . . waves rolling in and out . . . waves rolling in and out, helping you relax even further . . . even more relaxed than you are now . . . I'm going to stop talking for a few moments and allow you to concentrate all your attention on the waves coming up, folding back . . . coming closer and then receding . . . washing away with them any leftover feelings of worry or concern or tension or stiffness in your body.

When I begin speaking again it will not startle you, and you will notice the waves having washed away even more tension replaced by even more relaxation than you feel now. Good . . . even more relaxed . . . even more relaxed . . . in a moment when you feel ready to return to your normal state of awareness and alertness you can count yourself back fully awake and alert by counting backward from three to one . . . you can do this silently or you can allow yourself to go on relaxing . . . whichever you choose . . . keep remembering with each time you practice this exercise . . . each time you imagine waves rolling in and out . . . you are relaxing on the beach . . . this will allow your body to adapt to more comfortable and relaxing states . . . allowing you to get more deeply relaxed with each practice . . . when you're ready count yourself backward . . . awake, counting backward from three to one.

Relaxation Exercise Script I
Breathing

Close your eyes and begin breathing slowly and deeply in and out. Continue breathing slowly, deeply in and out. Let your body go limp. Let your muscles relax. Begin to allow the tension to drain out of your body. Any stiffness or tightness—let it release, dissipate. Begin to allow your mind to relax as well. Let go of your worries, concerns, and distractions. Let them fade out of your mind. In the same way that opening a window or a door lets smoke out of a smoky room and lets the air clear and become fresh, you can allow worries, concerns, and distractions to blow away. Feel those barriers, those impediments dissipate. As they fade away, just as if you could see that smoke dissipate, fade away and be replaced by fresh air, so, too, this elimination of worries and concerns allows your mind to feel fresh, open, and ready to be used for your benefit, ready to be used to help you do whatever it is that you wish to do as well as you can do it. As your mind clears, you have the opportunity to focus like a camera on any task or activity. The same way that you can focus the lens of a camera to be sharp and clear and to allow the camera to take pictures of perfect clarity, you can clear and focus your mind, your mind's eye, to allow you to perform like that camera. Just for a moment now let it appear in your mind's eye the perspective from the first tee. The same way that you adjust the lens on a camera, let your eyes focus and gaze out over the expanse, over the fairway in front of you. Notice how clearly you can see down the fairway. You can look down at your feet at one single blade of grass and see it clearly, clear and crisp.

Feel your club, your driver in your hand, and just for a moment look down at the head, notice how clearly you can see the grains of wood on the head of the driver. As your mind clears and your eyes focus with unusual clarity, notice the feel of the club in your hands. Notice how clearly you can feel the club in your hands. As your day progresses, you will notice how helpful that clarity of sight and that feel in your hands and arms is to help you throughout your round. In the same way that slow, deep breaths help your body and mind to relax, so, too, they help your clarity of vision, focus, and concentration. They help deepen that sense of feeling in your fingers and hands. You can feel as if the club is a part of you, an extension of your body, in the same way that you can move your arms, fingers, and hands any way, any direction you choose. So, too, will the club as an extension of your body do what your subconscious mind wishes it to do. Just as you've let the smoke clear out of your mind, and allowed clarity to replace it, along with that smoke as it left, along with it went any desire or means to try to control or think your way through your swing. Clearing up your mind allows a subconscious part down deep inside to take over, to do your wishes without your even asking. Clearing your mind and relaxing your body allows the automatic part of you to turn on and begin to direct or control your swing, your stroke, to allow these things to be executed, to be displayed without effort, without need to try to force the shot. With each slow, deep breath that you take as a trigger, the mechanisms inside are triggered to allow these things to happen, to unfold, to be carried out automatically, without thought. Trust that your body will carry these things out. Expect that your body will carry these things out easily, without thinking. In the same way that slow deep breaths deepen your relaxation, in the same way that clearing your mind allows you to mobilize and focus all of your mental energy on making the decisions that you want to make, your given choices, taking slow deep breaths allows the automatic part of you to take over and execute what you know, what you've done, and what you will do again with regularity. Now put your ball on the tee. Prepare yourself for your first shot. As you set up, take that slow deep breath. Allow your shot routine to unfold in your mind's eye and body.

Go ahead and take that first shot. Let your body feel the shot. Watch the ball travel, watch the flight. Watch it do what you wish it to do, expect it to do, know that it can do. Watch it land and roll. Notice how clearly you can see it despite its being so far away down the fairway. Allow that shot and all that made it be registered in your mind and body. To make it just a little easier, rehearse it again another time, and again another. Start down the course now. As you walk down the course, notice that you feel so relaxed and focused. That relaxation produces a feeling of lightness in your step, a spring to your step, almost as if you're floating down the course. You feel light, carefree, enjoying the moment, yet focused, concentrating, prepared. Let the second shot be a reflection of the first. Feel the club in your hands. Feel it a part of you. Know that it will do what you ask of it to do. Take a swing. Watch the ball float gently, quietly to the green, and land and roll as you envisioned in your mind's eye for the shot. Let it register and become part of you, making the next one just that much easier. Walk up to your ball on the green. Notice how easily, how clearly you can read the grain of the green, the contour, the break, in the same way that seeing in two dimensions differs from seeing in three and how more fully, completely you can see things in three dimensions, you will see these things on the green easily and clearly as if you're suddenly seeing in three dimensions. Feel the confidence that comes with the realization that you can see the putt much better than before. Feel the confidence that your positive experiences bring. Feel how good the putter feels in your hand as you line up, knowing that it will do what you ask of it. Feel the stroke and trust that your body and your self-conscious mind will carry out your bidding. Pull the trigger, watch the ball follow your line, the same line that you created in your mind's eye. Let it disappear. When you hear the sound of the ball in the cup, you'll know that you played the hole exactly as you wished, exactly as your body is capable, exactly as your self-conscious mind is capable because of your work, talent, and preparation. Trust that these things will happen. Expect them to happen. Feel down deep inside that they will happen, and they will happen.

Keep in mind that you can turn on all of these assets whenever you choose by taking slow and deep breaths. Breathing is like a switch that turns on these special skills of mind and body. Special skills that you have naturally and that you have fine-tuned and polished with your practice, experience, and dedication. Want it to happen, expect it to happen, and you make it happen. Want it to happen, expect it to happen, and it will happen. I'm going to stop talking now and allow you to return to your normal state of awareness, but a state of awareness that brings this knowledge and these skills with it, a state of awareness that brings with it a quiet, relaxed confidence in your ability to turn on these special talents to accomplish your goals. I will stop talking now and allow you to return at your own pace.

Relaxation Exercise Script II
Healing and Restoring, Round Replay, and Dismissal Practice

Breathe slowly and deeply. Let your breathing begin to trigger that chain of events inside your body and in your mind and allow you to release and let go. Breathe slowly and deeply, let your body relax. Let your mind clear, relax. Let it begin to drift and allow in a peaceful state of consciousness, peaceful, relaxed, breathing slow and deep, letting go of tension, letting aches and pains and stiffness drain out. Let it drain out of your body. Take along with it any concerns, worries or distractions. Begin to focus your mind's eye on my voice. You can let go of other sounds, distractions, sensations, thoughts, just let them peacefully drift off into the background, into the distance, and then gone completely. Gone completely. Now let go of the things that drain you, and take away your energy. Allow the creation of a state of mind and body that restores you, rebuilds you, re-focuses you, and re-energizes you. Just for a moment, allow your mind and body to enter that very receptive state. Just let this energy be absorbed. Let the strength return and build. Use your breathing to help you enter a state of mind and body that is much more restful than sleep. You can use it to take you to a place where your concentration can be pinpoint, sharp, and focused. You can use it to allow your muscles to heal and rest, to be restored from today's hard work that they carried out for you. You are in truth your body's keeper. You learn to relax and rest your body, to allow it to recover and be restored. You allow it to return quickly and heal to its most powerful and healthy state. You've learned to do this because like a marathon runner, you ask a lot of your body. You ask it to perform at a high level for hours on end, for days one after another. You can use your mind like a massage. Let your mind's eye just travel up and down your body. Let that focus pass up and down your body like a scanner. If you notice any spots of soreness or tightness, you can use the energy in your mind and your focus to unwind those tight muscles, like one who can unwind the knots in a rope. Let them unwind. As they unwind, the blood flows more freely. You can relax your body to a point where you almost can feel the blood flowing through your veins, arteries, bathing the tissue in comfortable healing fluid. Massage your body with your mind's eye, allow healing to take place, blood vessels open, dilated, the blood flowing freely and healing. Go all the way up and down your body, helping it relax further, and allowing it to recover from the day's demands.

Now take your mind's eye and focus on some of your best moments today, some of the moments where you felt the strongest, the most positive, the most in charge. Let your mind take you back in time to just a few hours ago. It may have been after you made a great shot or putt. It may have been after a great drive or approach shot. Pick one or two of these moments that are stored in your mind and let yourself just relish them, absorb them, bathe in them. Let them sink in and be absorbed. Let them become a part of you. Let them be stored in an accessible place, a place where you can access them, trigger them each time you wish by taking a slow and deep breath. You had many of those moments today. Just choose one or two that gave you particular satisfaction, that made you feel particularly good, joyful. Replay them in your mind's eye and let your body experience it—your body and mind experiencing it together. Let that rush of joy and good feelings travel up and down your body like energy moving, the energy that you felt as you made one good shot after another. As you return to these experiences, each time you return to them, even if it's just for a moment, notice how much more clearly you can see them in your mind's eye, how much more completely you can feel them in your body, in your hands, your arms, in your heart. Each time you visit these moments they became stronger and clearer because in the same way that you exercise your body, you take care of your body, you condition your body to be able to carry out what you ask of it, so too are you learning to exercise your mind, to strengthen your mind, to condition your mind to work for you, to let your mind be a tool at your disposal, to be another club in your bag to take out and use whenever you wish.

Just for a moment, I want you to take yourself back in time to the moment during the day that you were least happy about your shot, just for a moment, practice brushing it away, washing it away, letting it go, dismissing it as if it was nothing that concerned you, nothing to affect you. Just brush it off, just as you brush off a fly that might land on you. Notice that as you continue to strengthen and deepen your concentration, you continue to sharpen and use your mind to work for you, the mistakes or missed hits or moments that don't go as you might wish become nothing other than quick moments that dissipate, that disappear, are brushed off, and you move on. You'll find that these are instances that do not affect your recognition of your effort, of your experience, of your talents, and of your hard work. Each time you take a strong, deep breath and relax your mind and body further, you'll become more and more convinced that you're on a path that will allow you to reach your desired goals, and that each day you will take another step or two toward those goals. In addition, you will feel confident and gratified that you're taking the best steps, the right steps forward. You have not chosen an easy path. You have just chosen the most healthy and the most productive path in the long run.

In the same way that you could build a house, you can build your mind and body. In the same way that you build a house stone by stone, brick by brick, you can build a mental and physical set of skills and talents that will allow you to perform and execute at your very best, day in and day out, this week, next week, and weeks to come. Each time you practice this exercise, it will build on previous ones, like bricks, one put on top of another, to build your confidence, your purposefulness, and the certainty that you will achieve your goals. Want it to happen, expect it to happen, and you will make it happen. Want it to happen, trust that it will happen, and you will make it happen. Trust your mind and body. Trust what you have taught them. Trust the skills that you've fine-tuned and sharpened to a cutting edge. Trust that they will carry you forward. Trust they will uphold your confidence and your expectations. Want it to happen, expect it to happen, and you will make it happen. And while it's happening, enjoy it. Enjoy the fact that you're on the healthiest type of journey possible. Enjoy it along the way. I'm going to stop talking now, to allow you to return to a state of wakefulness, and alertness. You will return with increased confidence, a renewed sense of purpose and a peaceful serenity. You're going where you most want to go and you're well on your way to getting there. I will stop talking now to let you return at your own pace.

Relaxation Exercise Script III
Believe and Trust

Breathe slowly. Your mind and body are coming to recognize very easily a slow, deep, relaxed state of mind and body. When you breathe slowly and deeply, you may notice that it begins to get easier and easier with each practice to allow the tension, worry, to fade away, to dissipate. The body begins to recognize your request and respond easily and quickly, relaxing more quickly, easily, completely each time you practice. Breathe slowly and deeply so you can let go of the here and now, this moment. Just allow your mind and body to completely relax, to completely relax. Breathe slow and deep, let your body go limp. Let the last little bit of tension in the muscles drain out. Breathing slowly and deeply, you can keep those muscles relaxed and loose, whether it be your shoulders, your arms, your back or your legs, whether it's now or whether it's later, whether it's lying or standing, or even in a position where you're set up over a golf ball. One good slow deep breath triggers a deep relaxation that releases tension, a deep relaxation; let it work for you. Believe in your ability to produce a deep relaxation. Believe that you can produce it on the first tee today, on the first green, and on all those tees and greens thereafter. Your ability to relax will remain with you throughout the entire round. It will remain with you because you put in time and energy teaching your mind and body a deep state of relaxation and concentration. You are mastering your mind and body with your efforts and your practice. Believe in that developing skill. Trust that it will be there when you want it. Expect it to be there and it will be there.

A little later today you will walk up to the first tee, pick up your club, whether it's a driver, a fairway wood, or whatever club you use. With that club in hand, believe that it will accomplish all that you ask of it. As you grasp it in your hand, let it trigger in you the quiet confidence that comes with talent fine-tuned and heightened by years of hard work, practice and experience. In addition to your natural talents that you carry onto the first tee, you will also carry with you strength of mind and purpose, honed to a sharp edge by your practice and your efforts. You will bring to each shot the ability to display your talents and to perform it at your best, for you to enjoy. You bring with you experience on this course and many others, a knowledge and intelligence to make the tough decisions, to make them consistently, easily, in line with your strategy and your purpose. You bring with you an exceptional creativity that allows you to create a new, a totally different, and even a very difficult shot when needed to help yourself. All of these skills are in your bag like special clubs. When you feel that club in your hand, just let your mind and body be aware of all these special talents, skills, and assets that you bring. You can be confident that these things are present. You can use them out on the course. You bring with your the knowledge that this package of skills, this bag of clubs so full, is a significant advantage for you over the course and over other players. It allows you the wonderful opportunity to play well, even when you're not playing your absolute best. Believe in that extra ability, those extra skills. Trust that they're present. Expect them to come to your aid. You will allow yourself the opportunity to play without fear, and to play without the need to be perfect, to be exact. Want it to happen, expect it to happen. Believe that it will happen, and it will happen.

You will believe in yourself. You have a fundamental belief in yourself, a belief that if one works hard, works honestly, and does things in a positive way that good things will happen. Let yourself relax and play with all of these special clubs that you have available to you, some of which you were born with, some of which you have developed with hard work, some of which are there simply because of who you are, what you stand for, and how you go about living your life. Let this knowledge lighten your spirit. Let these facts carry you lightly, easily. These things will come to you just as taking slow, deep breaths triggers your awareness and your memory. Let that deep breath increase your confidence, let it deepen your trust that what you see the first time on the green or on the fairway is correct. Let it help you trust your judgment, your vision, your strategy. You will trust your decision, and realize that your first read or decision is best. You have no need to second-guess yourself at any time. Want it to happen, expect it to happen, believe that it will happen, and enjoy the wonderful experience as it happens.

I'm going to stop talking now, and allow you to take a moment and take yourself back to the day of your first round of gold, back to one of the moments that stands out in your mind. It may be a moment on the course after a good shot, or it may be a moment at some other time during the day, a moment where you felt especially joyful, especially light, happy. Just let yourself bathe in that experience for a moment to make it available to you, to bring it to the surface so you can benefit from the health and well-being, the strength, and the positive feelings that it produces. After you feel that you have soaked it up well, and made it available to you, remember that it will be easy to feel it again during your next round, by taking one of those slow, deep breaths. I'm going to stop talking now and allow you to simply enjoy that moment of experience.

Muscle Relaxation Script

OK, just settle back in your chair, and get as comfortable as you can. Let yourself relax to the best of your ability. Just relax... Now as you're relaxing like that, make a fist with your right hand. Clench your fist tighter and tighter. Bend your wrist down, keeping your fist clenched. Now feel the tension in your right hand. Feel the tension in your hand, your fist, and especially in your forearm . . . Now relax. Let your arm relax; let your fingers of your right hand become loose, and observe the contrast in the feelings in your arm. Now let yourself go, and try to become more relaxed all over . . . OK, now clench your fist again. Clench your fist very tight, bend your wrist down, hold it there, and notice the tension. Pay attention to the feelings . . . Now let go, relax; let your fingers straighten out, and notice the difference again. Just let it relax. . . . Relax. . . . Now repeat that with your left fist. Clench your left fist, and bend your wrist down . . . Now the opposite of tension, relax, and feel the difference. Continue relaxing like that for awhile.

Just continue to relax . . . Relax . . . Now clench both fists, very tight, both fists tense, your forearms tense, your wrists bent. Study the sensations. Study what they feel like. . . . Now relax. Relax. Straighten out your fingers, and feel the relaxation. Relax. Continue relaxing your hands and forearms more and more. More deeply relaxed; relax . . . Relax . . . Now, bend your arms; bend both arms at the elbows and tense your biceps. Tense them very hard. Bend your arms right up. Tense your biceps hard and study the tension. Study the tension in your biceps . . . OK, now let them relax. Let your hands drop down to the arms of the chair. Now feel the difference. Notice the difference between the tension and relaxation. Relax even further as you let the relaxation develop. Let it go even deeper . . . Relax . . . Now once more tense your biceps; hold the tension and observe the sensations associated with the tension carefully. Tense your biceps . . . Now relax. Just let yourself go as you enjoy the pleasant increasing sense of relaxation. There is nothing for you to do but continue to relax deeper and deeper, keeping in mind that relaxation is a positive process. Relaxation is doing nothing. Just relax. Nothing for you to do but to continue to relax. Relax. As you go on relaxing, pay close attention to the feelings in your muscles. Contrast the sensations of relaxation with those you experienced when you tensed your muscles . . . Now straighten your arms. Straighten them so you feel most tense in the triceps muscles along the back of your arms. Stretch your arms and feel the tension. Feel the tension in your triceps . . . Now relax. Relax. Get your arms back into a comfortable position. Let the relaxation proceed on its own. Your arms should feel comfortably heavy as you allow them to relax further and further. Now straighten your arms once more so that you feel the tension in the triceps muscles. Straighten them out and feel the tension . . . Now relax. Just let them go. Relax. Now let's concentrate on pure relaxation in your arms without any tension. Get your arms comfortable and let them relax further and further. Just continue relaxing your arms more and more. Even when your arms seem fully relaxed, try to let them relax even further. Keep in mind that relaxation is doing nothing as you try to achieve deeper and deeper levels of relaxation. Relax.

Now just let all of your muscles go loose and heavy. Just settle back quietly and comfortably. Enjoy the pleasant, easy, relaxed, heavy, comfortable feelings and sensation . . . Relax.

Now wrinkle up your forehead. Raise your eyebrows up. Wrinkle your forehead very tight. Make it tight . . . Now stop. Relax and smooth it out. Picture your forehead and scalp becoming smoother and

smoother as the relaxation increases. Smoother and smoother. Relax
. . . Now frown. Frown. Crease your brows. Frown hard and study the
tension again. Smooth out your forehead again. Just smooth it out,
and relax. Relax.

Now close your eyes very tight. Close them tight. Squeeze them
shut and feel the tension. Notice the sensation . . . Now relax. Relax
your eyes. Keep your eyes closed gently and notice the relaxation . . .
There's nothing for you to do but to go on relaxing . . . Relax.

Now clench your jaws. Bite your teeth together. Study the tension
throughout your jaws; especially in front of your ears . . . Now relax
your jaws. Relax. Let your lips part slightly and appreciate the
relaxation. Relax.

Now purse your lips. Press your lips together, tighter and
tighter . . . Relax. Note the contrast between tension and relaxation.
Feel the relaxation all over your face, all over your forehead and scalp,
eyes, jaws, lips, tongue, and throat. Just let the relaxation progress
further and further . . . Now tense your neck muscles. Press your head
back as far as it can go and feel the tension in your neck. Now roll your
head to the right and feel the tension shift. Now roll it to the left.
Straighten your head and bring it forward. Press your chin against
your chest. Now let your head return to a comfortable position, relax
and study the relaxation. Let the relaxation develop as you relax
further and further . . . Relax.

Now sit forward just a little and shrug your shoulders. Shrug your
shoulders back and up. Back and up. Hold the tension . . . OK, now drop
your shoulders and feel the relaxation. Relax your neck and shoulders
. . . Now shrug your shoulders again and move them around. Bring
them up, forward and back, and feel the tension in the shoulders and
upper back . . . OK, drop your shoulders again and relax . . . Relax . . .
Let the relaxation spread deep into your shoulders, right into your
back muscles. Relax your neck, and your throat, and your jaws, and
your face, as pure relaxation takes over and grows deeper, and deeper
. . . Now relax your whole body again to the best of your ability. Relax
your whole body. Feel the comfortable heaviness that accompanies
the relaxation. Breathing easily and freely, in and out; breathing easily
and normally. Notice how the relaxation increases as you exhale. As
you breathe out, just feel the relaxation as it spreads further and
further . . . Now take a deep breath and fill your lungs. Inhale deeply
and hold your breath. Study the tension . . . Now exhale. Let the walls
of your chest grow loose and push the air out automatically. Continue
relaxing and breathe freely and gently . . . Feel the relaxation and enjoy

it . . . That's fine. Now breathe out and appreciate the relief. Just breathe easily and normally as you continue relaxing your chest. Enjoy the warm, pleasant, comfortable sensations as you go on relaxing. Relax . . . Let the relaxation spread to your back, shoulders, neck, and arms. Just let go and enjoy the relaxation . . . Relax.

From now on when you tense your muscles, breathe in and hold your breath with the tension. When you relax the muscles, breathe out and then continue breathing easily and freely as you continue to relax further and further.

Now let's pay attention to your abdominal muscles. Tighten your stomach muscles. Make your abdomen hard. Notice the tension, and now relax. Let your muscles loosen, and note the contrast . . . Now again tighten your stomach muscles. Hold the tension and study it . . . Now relax. Notice the general feeling of well-being that comes when you relax your stomach . . . Relax . . . Now pull your stomach in. Pull the muscles right in and feel the tension this way . . . Now relax again. Let your stomach out. Continue breathing normally and easily, feeling the gently messaging action all over your chest and your stomach. Now pull your stomach in again, and hold the tension. Now push out the tense that way. Hold the tension . . . Now pull in and feel the tension. And now relax. Relax your stomach fully. Let the tensions dissolve. Let the relaxation grow deeper and deeper. Each time you breathe out, notice the rhythmic relaxation, both in your lungs and in your stomach. Notice how your chest and stomach relax more and more when you breathe out. Try and let go of all contractions anywhere in your body. Just relax all over . . . Relax . . . Now let's go to your lower back. Make your lower back hollow, and feel the tension along your spine . . . OK, settle down comfortably again. Relax your lower back. . . . Relax . . . Now arch your back. Arch your back and feel the tension. Try to keep the rest of your body as relaxed as you can. Try to localize the tension in your lower back. . . . OK, relax again. Relaxing further and further, less tension everywhere . . . Relax your lower back. Relax your upper back and spread the relaxation across the chest, shoulders, arms and face. Let these areas relax further and further. Let them relax deeper and deeper. Let go of all tensions and relax. . . . Relax your whole body further as you enjoy the pleasant, warm, comfortable feelings of relaxation as they spread and deepen . . . Relax . . . Now flex your thighs. Flex your thighs by pressing down against the floor with your feet. Press down against the floor and feel the tension in your thighs and your upper legs . . . OK, relax. Relax and note the differences in the feelings and sensations of the relaxation compared to the tension . . . Now tense your thighs again. Push down against the floor. Feel the tension in your thighs . . . OK, relax. Relax. Let the relaxation proceed on its own. Let it spread. Let it spread on up your body. Relax. All right, now press your feet and toes down and away from you so that your calves become tense. Make your calf muscles tense and study the tension. OK, relax. Relax your calves as you enjoy the pleasant, warm, comfortable feelings of relaxation. There's nothing for you to do but to just relax. Relax.

Now bend your toes up. Bend your toes up as far as you can so that you feel tension along your shins. Feel the tension along your shins . . . Now relax. Just relax . . . Keep relaxing . . . Let yourself relax further all over. Relax your feet, your ankles, your calves, your shins, knees, thighs, and your hips. Feel the pleasant heaviness of your lower body as you relax still more. Now spread the relaxation to your stomach, your waist, and your lower back. Let go more and more, further and further. Feel the relaxation all over. Let it go on up to your upper back, your chest, your shoulders, and arms, and right on down to the very tips of your fingers. Relax . . . Keep relaxing more and more deeply. Make sure no tension has crept into your throat. Relax your neck and your jaws and all your facial muscles. Keep relaxing your whole body like that for a while. Let yourself relax. Relax.

Now you can become even more relaxed than you are merely by taking in a deep breath and slowly exhaling. With your eyes closed so that you become less aware of objects and movements around you, breathe in deeply and feel yourself becoming heavier. Take in a long deep breath and then let it out very slowly . . . Feel how heavy and relaxed you have become. Just relax. Relax. In a state of perfect relaxation you should feel unwilling to move a single muscle in your body . . . Now think about the effort that would be required to raise your right arm. As you think about raising your right arm, see if you can notice any tension that might have crept into your shoulder and your arm. Now you decide not to lift the arm, but to continue relaxing. Observe the relief and the disappearance of the tension.

OK, just continue relaxing like that. Relax. OK, now when you feel like getting up, count backwards from three to one. You should feel fine and refreshed, wide-awake, and calm . . . OK, let's count. One, wiggle your toes and legs. Two, open your eyes and turn your head from side to side. Three, sit up . . . Everyone feeling fine, refreshed, wide-awake, and calm.

index

about the authors

A clinical psychologist in private practice since 1978, **Wayne R. Glad, PhD**, added a new twist when he became a sport psychology and performance enhancement consultant in 1990. Since then, he has consulted with professional, college, and high school teams in golf, football, basketball, baseball, tennis, swimming, wrestling, and ice skating.

In 1997, Glad presented ground-breaking research in optimal mental preparation for peak performance golf to the Association for the Advancement of Applied Sports Psychology in San Diego. Making his home in Glendale, Wisconsin, Glad currently serves as a sport psychology and performance enhancement consultant to the PGA Tour players and the Marquette University golf team, the USA Junior Golf Association, and the David Leadbetter Junior Golf camps.

When he's not improving the psyche of the world's top golfers, Glad enjoys home-schooling his 12-year-old twins, traveling, scuba diving, and hitting the links himself.

One of the PGA Tour's most successful golfers—ranking in the top 25 all-time money winners—**Chip Beck** has seen his name consistently reaching the leader board throughout the 80's and early 90's.

Co-record holder for the lowest score ever shot in a PGA Tour event—a 59—Beck has won four PGA Tour events, placed second in three of the PGA Tour's Majors (at the U.S. Open in 1986 and 1991 and the Masters in 1993). Beck played on three Ryder Cup teams and has solidified himself as one of the top U.S. players over the past 20 years.

A true student of the game, Beck has co-authored several articles for *Golf Digest* and serves as Director of the Western Golf Association. When away from the tour, Beck likes spending time with his family, playing paddle tennis, landscaping, and gardening. He lives in Lake Forest, Illinois, just north of Chicago.

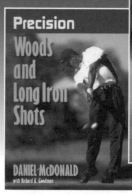
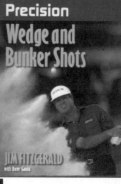
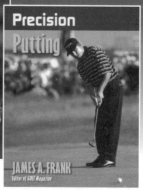